# The gar

*of Christ*

# The garments *of Christ*

IAN R. K. PAISLEY

AMBASSADOR
Belfast • Greenville

**The garments** *of Christ*



This edition 1996



ISBN 1 898787 72 7

Published by

**AMBASSADOR PRODUCTIONS, LTD.**

Providence House
16 Hillview Avenue,
Belfast, BT5 6JR

Emerald House
1 Chick Springs Road, Suite 102
Greenville, South Carolina, 29609

# Foreword

**THE WARDROBE OF CHRIST!** The garments of Christ! The wonderful raiment of our wonderful Lord! What a theme! I know of no other book which covers this tremendous subject, and therefore I am sending forth this work yet again.

The chapters are sermonic in form. They were prepared and delivered from the pulpit of Martyrs Memorial Free Presbyterian Church, Belfast, amidst a large and busy city pastorate, and whilst discharging a heavy load of pastoral and political duties.

The recordings of these expositions have had a very wide circulation already. No effort has been made to alter either style, substance or presentation. They go forth as they were delivered.

Their preparation was a blessing. Their proclamation was a blessing, and I trust their further publication in this form will also be a blessing.

May He who put on and off the garments of which they speak, be pleased to use them to His honour and glory.

Yours,
'Set for the Defence of the Gospel'
Ian R.K. Paisley
Eph 6:19+20

*February 1996*

Martyrs Memorial Free Presbyterian Church
356-376 Ravenhill Road,
Belfast, BT6 8GL
Northern Ireland.

# Contents


1. **The distinctive garments** *of Christ* ........ 9
2. **The distinguished garments** *of Christ* ........ 17
3. **The distinguished garments** *of Christ* (continued) ........ 27
4. **The distinguished garments** *of Christ* (continued) ........ 39
5. **The distinguished garments** *of Christ* (continued) ........ 47
6. **The distinguished garments** *of Christ* (concluded) ........ 57
7. **The disdained garments** *of Christ* ........ 69
8. **The discarded garments** *of Christ* ........ 81
9. **The discarded garments** *of Christ* (continued) ........ 91
10. **The discarded garments** *of Christ* (concluded) ........ 103
11. **The crown** *of thorns* ........ 113
12. **The many crowns** *of Christ* ........ 127

# 1 The distinctive garments of Christ

**EVERY TRUE BORN-AGAIN** child of God can re-echo the words of the apostle Peter concerning Christ, "Unto you therefore, who believe He is precious". To the believer, everything which concerns his Lord is precious. The *Person* of the Saviour is precious. The *Place* which the Saviour occupied in the eternity that is past, and now occupies in the glory of His kingdom, is precious. His *Purpose* "to bring many sons into glory" is precious. Yes and when we stand under the shadow of the cross, and lift our eyes to behold the suffering Son of God, His *Passion* is especially precious.

But while those great things, essential things, and more important things demand and deserve the contemplation of the people of God, yet some of the things which we do not often contemplate are equally precious, simply because they have to do with our Blessed Saviour.

I want to take for my subject "The Wardrobe of Christ" and for my text that part of the first verse of Isaiah chapter sixty three, "Glorious in His apparel". His garments most surely must be most precious to His people.

## SWEET SMELLING

Psalm forty-five and verse eight, "All thy garments smell of myrrh and aloes and cassia". The garments of Christ are sweet smelling, they are perfumed with the scent of heaven and the odours of the Godhead.

Old Bishop Horsley said:

"Now the perfumed garments of the psalmist's King denote the very same thing which was typified under the law by the perfumed garments of the high priest; the psalmist's King being indeed the real person of whom the high priest, in every particular of his office, his services, and his dress, was the type. The perfumed garments were typical first of the graces and virtues of the Redeemer Himself in His human character; secondly, of whatever is refreshing, encouraging, consoling and cheering, in the external ministration of the word; and thirdly, of the internal comforts of the Holy Bible. But the incense fumed upon the golden altar was typical of a far inferior, though of a precious and holy thing - namely, of whatever is pleasing to God in the faith, the devotions, and the good works of the saints. Now the psalmist says that the fragrance breathing from the garments of the King far excels not only the sweetest odours of any earthly monarch's palace but that it surpasses those spiritual odours of sanctity in which the King himself delights. The consolations which the faithful under all their sufferings receive from Him, in the example of His holy life, the ministration of the word and sacraments, and the succours of the Spirit, are far beyond the proportion of anything they have to offer in return to Him, in their praises, their prayers, and their good lives; notwithstanding in these their services He condescends to take delight. This is the doctrine of this highly mystic text, that the value of all our best works of faith and obedience, even in our own eyes, must sink into nothing when they are contrasted with the exuberant mercy of God extended to us through Christ." Such is the fragrance breathing from the great King's wedding garment.

## BLOOD STAINED

Not only are the garments of Christ sweet smelling but they are blood stained. The teaching in Isaiah chapter sixty-three is that the blood of His enemies stain His garments. Verse three: "their blood shall be sprinkled upon my garments". But not only is the blood of His enemies sprinkled upon His garments, but our blessed Saviour (as we shall see as we continue) wears a vesture that is dipped in His own most precious blood. So the garments of Christ, to the eye of faith, are hallmarked with the blood of our redemption.

In this message we are going to approach the robing room of the King of kings. We are going to unlock the Wardrobe of Christ. As we examine garment by garment, I trust that we will not only learn the lessons God would have us learn, but I pray that in our contemplation, we shall breathe the fragrance and the perfume of those garments and worship the One who condescended to don them for and on our behalf.

**FOUR TYPES OF GARMENTS**

The first garments of Christ, which I want to refer to, I would call "The Distinctive Garments of Christ."

The second garments of Christ I would call "The Distinguished Garments of Christ."

The third set of garments I would call "The Disdained Garments of Christ."

Then next I want to contemplate "The Discarded Garments of Christ".

He laid certain garments aside forever at the tomb, for He needed them no more.

Let me deal with the first set of garments which I have called "The Distinctive Garments of Christ." These are peculiar to Him but with a special message for us all.

Luke's gospel chapter two and verse seven, and having looked at that verse, then compare it with verse twelve. Luke's gospel chapter two tells of the Nativity, the Birth of the Saviour. Here we read of His virgin mother; "She brought forth her first-born son, and wrapped Him in swaddling clothes."

I want you to notice the expression, it is very important, "wrapped Him in swaddling clothes, and laid Him in a manger." Note the reason "because there was no room for them in the inn". Now verse twelve: "And this shall be a sign unto you; ye shall find the babe wrapped in swaddling clothes, lying in a manger".

Now there was both a concealing and a revealing in this Distinctive Garment which He wore after He was born.

**ONE: WHAT THOSE CLOTHES REVEALED**

Those garments which His virgin mother took and wrapped Him in were most significant, because instead of being the garments of life, they were the garments of death. It was a winding sheet which she used when He was born just the same sheet which was used when He was wrapped for His burial. The whole significance of His birth has a direct parallel with His bleeding and the whole significance of the crib has a direct parallel with the cross.

Where was this stable? It was cut out of the rock in the hillside; it was a cave; it was like the sepulchre where at the last He was laid.

Further, it was the place of the food for the beast. And what shall I say of the sepulchre where the great beast of death lurked? It makes food of the human body. Yes, there is a direct parallel between His birth and His bleeding and between His crib and His cross.

**BORN TO DIE**

So, first of all, we have revealed to us in these garments that He was born to die.

The first garment which pressed upon His baby body was a garment which spoke of death.

He did not come to live forever upon this world. He did not come to live out the aeons of eternal life traversing our planet. He came with one objective, with one great goal: "Who for the joy that was set before Him, endured the cross."

As I peer into the straw, a babe is there. What babe is this? It is a babe wrapped in swaddling clothes, with the shroud of death already pressing on His little body. This was the revelation which those clothes brought forth.

**BORN POOR**

Secondly it was a revelation of poverty. Notice what the verse says, "she wrapped Him in swaddling clothes". No midwife there to assist her in the agonies of childbirth. No gentle woman's hand to console her as she brought forth her first-born son. Jesus Christ was born in the circumstances of abject poverty. He who was King of kings, was born in the same way as a pauper's child was born. The only hand that was to clothe Him was the hand of a virgin. There is a great significance in this, because only a virgin's hand was fit to clothe the virgin body of my Saviour. Any other hand would be a hand unfitted for that task.

## HANDLING CHRIST'S BODY

If you study the scriptures you will find that the body of Christ had times of preservation, when no hand touched it but the hand of the believer. This was true at His birth. It was a believer's hand which clothed Him at His birth, Mary, who had already said that she rejoiced in God her Saviour.

It was two believers who clothed Him for His burial, Joseph of Arimathaea and Nicodemus. In between His birth and death evil hands were to tear His clothes, part His garments, buffet, beat and blacken His blessed body. At His birth it was the hands of a believer which wrapped Him in the swaddling clothes. Yes, and at His death it was the hands of believers that prepared Him for the burial.

## BORN TO BE SACRIFICED

Thirdly, it was a revelation of His passion.

He came to die, my blessed Saviour! He is God incarnate. Oh the mystery, the tremendous mystery of it all; that the eternal God, incarnate in a babe's form should lie in swaddling clothes. The very first cloth which touched the Eternal Word made flesh, was the cloth of death. Here we have His passion, He wore not the broidered garments of a prince. Aye and no garment woven on earth was fit or glorious enough to wrap around Him. Instead it was the shroud. It was the garment of the sepulchre. It was the trappings of the tomb. The shadow of the cross was over His whole life, "I must be about my Father's business" was the first recorded words He ever spoke. Yes and let me repeat it, the first cloth that touched Him was the cloth of death.

## TWO: WHAT THOSE CLOTHES CONCEALED

There was a great concealing here. There have been great events which we have all waited for in this world. The whole world waited for that event. But here was an event greater than any other event that would ever take place in the history of mankind and God concealed it.

Notice the word "wrapped". If you want to cover up something, you wrap it up! And God has hidden this from the wise and prudent, and revealed it unto babes. "If the princes of this world had known," said Paul, "they would not have crucified the Lord of glory". They would not have done it, but they did not know, for God wrapped it up. It was only those elected by the covenant of everlasting grace, who would know the mystery of it all. For He has not revealed it to the wise or prudent, but He has revealed it unto babes, the new born ones, the ones that have entered into His kingdom by that great and spiritual birth.

## THREE: THE GARMENT WITH THE HEM

But come a little further in Matthew's gospel. Turn over (keeping in mind "The Distinctive Garments of Christ") to Matthew chapter nine. In Matthew chapter nine, we have a woman, (verse 20).

"And, behold, a woman, which was diseased with an issue of blood twelve years, came behind Him, and touched the hem of His garment: For she said within herself, If I may but touch His garment, I shall be whole."

The hem of His garment. The women folk know that the hem of the garment is the last thing that is done. It is the finishing and finished work.

Now there are three things about the hem I want to point out, remembering this is the Distinctive Garment of Christ, distinctive in that its whole emphasis is upon death.

The hem is made by the turning up of the extremity of the garment.

In His finished work, Jesus Christ, having lived thirty-three years, turned up the end of His life to God. If you study John's gospel you should mark how many times the word "lifted up" occurs. "If the Son of man be lifted up". All that Jesus Christ was, and everything He did in the fulfilling of the law, as our substitute and surety on the cross was turned up to the gaze of heaven. He offered Himself without spot unto God.

To make the hem, one not only turns up the garment but one must also pierce the garment with a needle. There must be the piercing of that turned up cloth. Here we have in type the piercing of the tree, not with a needle but with cruel nails, not with fine pointed steel but with jagged spear. That was how my Lord finished this great work.

There was a hem upon His garment, the finished work upon His clothing. At the cross He finished the work God gave Him to do.

There is something else necessary to the making of the hem. It must be a threaded needle.

The thread must enter where the piercing is taking place.

Following the needle there must come the thread, and that thread speaks to me of the unbroken purpose of God. The golden thread which runs from eternity to eternity, the golden unbroken thread of the divine purpose that God should redeem from among the sons of men a people for His Name.

So the garment is finished. The hem is made. The robe has been turned up. The needle has done its piercing. The thread has done its fixing. There is just one thing needed for you and for me. We must touch the hem of His garment. Christ was there. The poor diseased woman was there. "If I touch His hem, I will be made whole."

*She only touched the hem of His garment,*
*As to His side she stole,*
*Amid the crowd that gathered around Him,*
*And straightway she was whole.*

*Oh touch the hem of His garment*
*And thou too shall be free,*
*His saving power this very hour*
*Shall bring God's life to thee.*

"The Distinctive Garments of Christ". The first garment that ever pressed His baby body was the clothing of the death shroud.

# 2 The distinguished garments *of Christ*

**ISAIAH CHAPTER SIXTY-THREE** and verse one: "Who is this that cometh from Edom, with dyed garments from Bozrah? This that is glorious in apparel, travelling in the greatness of His strength? I that speak in righteousness mighty to save". Note the little clause 'This that is glorious in his apparel'. We have been taking that scripture sentence as the basis for this series of sermons which I have called 'The Wardrobe of Christ'.

In the first sermon we dealt with the Distinctive Garments of Christ. We considered the swaddling clothes and the garment with the hem, which speaks of the finished work of our wonderful Lord. We go on to meditate upon the Distinguished Garments of Christ.

The Old Testament prophets all had an eye to the great sacrifice of the Cross. It is noticeable that in the Mosaic ceremonies, great detail is given concerning every sacrifice that was to be offered. So every detail about the death of Christ and His crucifixion upon the cross is worthy of the careful study of God's people, and it is when we come to the cross that we have told us by each Gospel writer, Matthew, Mark, Luke and John, something peculiar about the garments of Christ.

Now I will be dealing, as I continue this series, with what I am calling "The Disdained Garments of Christ" with special reference to His death. But if you turn to John's gospel chapter nineteen, you will find if you compare John's gospel with the other gospels commonly known as the synoptic gospels, Matthew, Mark and Luke that only John goes into this matter with great detail.

Reading at verse twenty-three in John chapter nineteen: "Then the soldiers, when they had crucified Jesus, took His garments and made four parts, to every soldier a part; and also His coat: now the coat was without seam, woven from the top throughout. They said therefore among themselves, Let us not rend it, but cast lots for it, whose it shall be: that the scripture might be fulfilled, which saith, They parted My raiment among them, and for My vesture they did cast lots. These things therefore the soldiers did."

Here we have some intimate details about the Distinguished Garments of Christ. I believe that the garments He wore in the day of His humiliation were distinguished.

As we continue our study, we will turn over to the first chapter of the book of Revelation and if you glace at that chapter you will discover that there we have some of the Distinguished Garments of our blessed risen Lord. Revelation chapter one and verse thirteen: "... the Son of Man clothed with a garment down to the foot, and girt about the paps with a golden girdle". Here is the high priestly garment of our wonderful risen Lord.

Then if you go further over in the book of the Revelation you will find the garment of Christ at His coming. We will be looking at that garment also. It is an edifying study. Revelation chapter nineteen: "And He was clothed with a vesture dipped in blood: and His Name is called the Word of God." I might say there is another garment which is a Distinguished Garment "He laid aside His garments and girt Himself with a towel" John 13:4. He took the place of a servant in the day of His humiliation. Oh this is a wonderful study, well worthy of the blessed meditation of God's people.

We are now going to look at those garments which He wore habitually, His everyday garments. I want to speak first of their *Glory*, secondly of their *Number*, thirdly of their *Significance* and lastly of their *Disposal*.

## THEIR GLORY

The glory of these garments was not inherent in them. We repudiate the idolatrous blasphemy of the Church of Rome that claims that they still possess some of the garments of Christ.

Their glory was an acquired glory. It was theirs because of the One who wore them, their glory is essentially the Lord's. They were just the plain garments worn by any poor Galilean, but there was a glory that shone into them and through them because it was our blessed Lord who wore them.

You will remember that one day three men saw how glorious those garments were. They went up into a mountain with the Lord, known as the Mount of Transfiguration. Now turn over with me in your Bible and watch very carefully, because every word is important and if you miss a word you will miss the vision and consequently miss the blessing. Matthew seventeen and verse one: "And after six days Jesus taketh Peter, James and John his brother and bringeth them up into an high mountain apart, And was transfigured before them: and His face did shine as the sun, and His raiment was white as the light."

Now bear particular attention to the description of His raiment. It was white as the light. That is Matthew's narrative. Turn with me now to Mark chapter nine, and there in Mark's gospel you will find something different. Mark nine, verse two and three "And after six days Jesus taketh with Him Peter, and James, and John, and leadeth them up into an high mountain apart by themselves: and He was transfigured before them. And His raiment became shining, exceeding white as snow; so as no fuller on earth can white them."

Notice the difference between Matthew and Mark.

Turn with me to Luke's narrative. Luke chapter nine, verses twenty-eight and twenty nine: "And it came to pass about an eight days after these sayings, He took Peter and John and James and went up into a mountain to pray. And as He prayed, the fashion of His countenance was altered, and His raiment was white and glistering." There is a difference between them all. I hope you have noted the difference.

First of all Matthew says, "white as light"; Mark says, "white as snow; so as no fuller on earth can whiten them"; and Luke says, "His raiment was white and glistering".

That word "glistering" occurs only once in the whole of the New Testament, this is the only place it occurs, and it means flashing as lightning. The garments of Christ! Why this difference? This difference is very significant, because it brings out very clearly the three-fold offices of the Lord Jesus Christ. Those of you who were brought up on the Shorter Catechism will know, and those of you who were not should get a copy and study it. It will be good for you! The Shorter Catechism asks the question "What offices doth Christ execute as our Redeemer?" The answer is, "Christ as our Redeemer executeth the offices of a Prophet, Priest and King, both in His estate of humiliation and exaltation". Prophet, Priest and King. The garments of Christ in Matthew reveal Him as the Prophet, look at it: "white as light" . Is not that what a prophet comes to do, to give us God's light, to enlighten our eyes, to throw God's light upon His Word. And in His transfiguration He appeared in the garments of the Prophet, plain Galilean home-spun garments but through the glory of Christ they are transformed into garments "white as light".

The second office that Jesus Christ executed is the office of a priest. What is the purpose of a priest? The purpose of a priest is to bring cleansing. Note the significance of Mark 9:3. He said the garments were "white as snow" and then he makes this contrast and says "as no fuller on earth could white them". Here we have the priest standing in the garments of his priestly cleansing power. Notice the two similes that are used; snow and fullers earth. Fullers earth is the cleansing of earth. Snow comes from heaven, no man's hand ever formed it, it comes pure from the blue sky of glory. Praise God, our great High Priest does not cleanse us with a cleansing that is man-made, "Though your sins be as scarlet, they shall be as white as snow". So you have Christ as the priest.

But notice something very peculiar. In Matthew it is six days, in Mark it is six days but when you come to Luke it is eight days. There is a change you know. Now compare and see, it is very important. After six days on the seventh day, the Sabbath day, He is Prophet and He is Priest. Turn to Luke's gospel chapter nine and verse twenty-nine, and there it is about eight days after. Is there a mistake? No there are no mistakes in the Word of God. Luke is taking his timing from the sayings of Christ, not from the one particular saying recorded in Matthew and Mark. A different aspect of Christ however, is coming out of it. The eighth day is the day after the seventh day, the day is which Jesus rose from the dead.

Jesus Christ was not seen in His humiliation as the King. If the princes of this world had known, they would not have crucified the Lord of Glory. Turn with me to Matthew chapter twenty and have a look at verse twenty-seven "For as the lightning cometh out of the east, and shineth even unto the west; so shall also the coming of the Son of man be." His raiment was white and flashing as lightning. On the eighth day He is resurrected. It was the day when He entered into His glory. It was the day that preceeded His ascension, and praise God it is the day which marks His coming in power and great glory. Men do not see the King today but one day they will see Him.

My blessed Lord, despised, rejected and reviled, is King of Kings and Lord of Lords, and His raiment is white like flashing lightning. That is the glory of the Distinguished everyday garments of Christ.

**THEIR NUMBER**

In reading the scriptures one would say (I am referring to verse twenty-three and twenty four of John's gospel) that they tore all the clothes of Christ into four parts, but when they came to the fifth garment, because it was woven from the top throughout, they did not tear it because of its construction. That however is not the meaning of this verse.

You must go back to Psalm twenty-two. This Psalm, of course, is a great Messianic prophecy. Psalm twenty-two and verse eighteen, "They part My garments among them". The word "part" does not mean to rend, it means to "apportion" to give a particular portion to each person. This brings out the precious truth of the garments of Christ. Because the Galilean peasant had five garments. He had his sandals, he had his headdress, he had his outward cloak, he had his girdle, and he had his inner coat, five in all. And so the four soldiers got one garment apiece. One got the sandals. One got the girdle. One got the headdress and one got the outer cloak. Then they came to the coat, which was the garment worn next to the flesh. It was the removal of that garment that made our Lord stark naked on the Cross. We will talk about the significance of that when we come to the Discarded Garments of Christ.

You will of course remember fallen Adam. God clothed him. But the last Adam was unclothed so that we might be clothed in the garment of His imputed righteousness. We will however also come to that. It is a wonderful study.

There were five garments. A portion of His garments was given to each soldier, the sandals, the girdle, the outward cloak and the headdress. The seamless robe remained, which makes a wonderful study in itself. Five is an interesting number in scripture. Five is made up of four and one. Four is the number of the world - "the four corners of the earth", "the four great seas", and "the four winds of heaven." We read about them in the Bible. Four is the number of the world, and if you go back to Genesis you will find that the material world was completed in four days.

One in scripture stands for God, the one true God, the unity of the Godhead. So the world (4) and God (1) that is, God intervening in the world, make five - that is grace. So when you read the Bible look for every five, there are a lot of them and you will find that five is the number of grace.

If you take it another way five is made up of three and two. Three in scripture is the number of fullness. If I want to know the fullness of this building I need three numbers, I need length, breadth and height. By multiplying these I get the cubic capacity. Three is the number of fullness, there are three persons in the Godhead. Two is the number of Christ, He is the second person. "And it pleased the Father that in Him should all fullness dwell". John's gospel chapter one: "He is full of grace". Three and two make five and five is the number of grace. You can go through the Bible and find this out for yourself. Study it.

So these five garments speak of grace. Everything about Christ speaks about grace. Grace is the free, undeserved, unmerited favour of God freely bestowed. It is more than love, it is love set absolutely free in triumph over the heart of man in his sin and in his depravity.

## THEIR SIGNIFICANCE

Now the first four garments mentioned were the garments that were seen of men. Men saw the sandals, they saw the headdress, they saw the outward cloak and they saw the girdle. Now what do these four garments represent? Well, I think that it is quite evident that they represent what men saw about the Lord.

How do I know what men saw about the Lord? I can only know as I read the four gospels. The four gospels are records which tell me what men saw about the Lord. Matthew depicts the Lord Jesus Christ as Sovereign: "Where is He that is born King of the Jews?" That is the question at the beginning. Mark shows me Jesus the Servant. There is no genealogy in Mark. Nobody worries who is the father, mother, grandfather or grandmother of a servant. He is just the servant in Mark. In Luke He is the Saviour. Luke depicts Him as the Saviour. John depicts Him as the Son.

These four garments bring us Christ as Sovereign, Servant, Saviour and Son. Now look at them: Of course the girdle is the badge of office. The prophetic office was marked by a leathern girdle. Turn over to 2 Kings 1:8 and compare it with Matthew 3:4 and you will see that John the Baptist had a leathern girdle about his loins.

### The girdle speaks of Christ the Sovereign

Do you remember that lovely character Jonathan? He gave David everything, (I Samuel eighteen verse four), down to his girdle. The girdle was the badge of his princely office. If you turn over to 2 Samuel 6:14 you will find that David wore an ephod as a girdle when as the king he marched in the procession which brought the ark of the covenant to Jerusalem. The girdle is the badge of office. The Lord Jesus Christ had the girdle. Men did not see it then as the girdle of kingship. But if you turn over with me to Revelation chapter one verse thirteen you will notice that in that high priestly garb that Jesus wears, it says that he was "girt about the paps with a golden girdle". So the girdle speaks to me of Christ the sovereign.

### The sandals speak of Christ the Servant

It is easy to see that the sandals speak of Christ the Servant. The sandals of service. Turn with me to Isaiah chapter fifty-two, and there we have a wonderful word. Verse seven says, "How beautiful upon the mountains are the feet of him that bringeth good tidings, that publisheth peace". How beautiful are the feet! If you want an interesting study go to the gospels and mark everywhere that Jesus walked.

Some day when I have time I am going to preach a series of sermons on the various postures of Christ: Where He lay, Where He stood, Where He walked. You know one day He walked up and down in the Courts of the Temple and it was winter. Do you know what it says? "He walked briskly". Yes, my Saviour was cold. He had not enough garments to keep warmth in His body. The blessed Saviour in winter time walked briskly to keep the blood in perfect circulation. He Who was rich, yet for our sakes became poor. These are wonderful things about the Lord, worthy of our study. Those sandals speak to me of the gospel of Mark, He is the Servant.

### The outer garment speaks of Christ as Saviour

Next the outer garment - a wonderful study is this garment with the hem on it. It is the garment that the woman touched, but the woman was not the only one that touched the hem of His garment. Turn with me to Matthew chapter fourteen and verse thirty-six, and what does it say there? "And besought Him that they might only touch the hem of His garment: and as many as touched were made perfectly whole". That garment speaks of Christ as Saviour.

## The headdress speaks of the concealment of His Deity

Now all we have left is the headdress, and that is very important. It is the headdress that conceals the man of the East. Do you ever wonder why they gave thirty pieces of silver to Judas to betray Him? The Lord Jesus walked in and out of the Temple frequently. He was a well known character. I will tell you why, because once the headdress went on, all that was seen were the eyes, the nose and part of the lip, and there were thousands of men who were of the same stature as the Lord in Jerusalem at that time, and so they needed someone to identify Him.

I remember Mr. Mullan of Lurgan telling us that when he was in the East he dressed himself up in Arab garments and put on the headdress. As he was walking down the street he saw his friend Mr. Irvine of Newcastle, and he gave him a hit on the ribs. Mr. Irvine looked at him and said, "What are you doing?" and he pushed him again, and his friend thought he was being attacked by some Arab guerilla. The headdress effectually disguised him. It is a concealment.

Listen, here is Christ the Messiah. "Let this mind be in you that was also in Christ Jesus, Who being in the form of God thought it not robbery to be equal with God, but made himself of no reputation and took upon Him the form of a servant and being found in fashion as a man; humbled himself and became obedient unto death even the death of the Cross." If they had known they would not have crucified the Lord of glory. Yes, His headdress speaks to me of the concealment of His Deity. The Word became flesh and dwelt among us.

I want you to think about the seamless robe of Christ. I want you to meditate on this thought, "it is woven from the top throughout," woven from the top.

You see it was the garment nearest to the flesh. It was usually of white linen fastened around the neck and coming right down covering the whole body. A seamless robe. Ask the Lord to let you know what that robe means.

You know some ecumenists talk about the seamless robe of Christ as if that robe represented the visible church. It represents no such thing. That robe represents something far more precious than church organisation. Think about it.

Do you remember the man who came in and the king said, "Why have you not on the wedding garment?" Blessed are those that are called to the marriage supper of the Lamb. "Bring the best robe and put it on him". "If there be any virtue, think on these things."

# 3 The distinguished garments *of Christ*

## PART TWO

**JOHN'S GOSPEL CHAPTER NINETEEN** verses twenty-three and twenty-four: "Then the soldiers, when they had crucified Jesus, took His garments, and made four parts, to every soldier a part; and also His coat; now the coat was without seam, woven from the top throughout. They said therefore among themselves, Let us not rend it, but cast lots for it, whose it shall be: that the scripture might be fulfilled, which saith, They parted my garments among them, and for my vesture they did cast lots."

We are continuing our meditation upon "The Wardrobe of Christ". We have dealt with the distinctive garments of Christ; the swaddling clothes, speaking of death, and the garment with turned up hem, speaking of the finished work. We have already looked at the four garments, the sandals, the headdress, the outer robe and the girdle.

We come now to consider one of the most precious of all subjects in regard to the garments of Christ. We come to consider the seamless robe, or the vesture or the inner garment, the garment that pressed close to the Saviour's flesh.

This garment has some tremendous lessons for us, and I believe it will bring in its contemplation blessing to all our hearts. Now look again at verses twenty-three and twenty-four: "Then the soldiers, when they had crucified Jesus, took His garments and made four parts". You notice these parts did not consist of rending the garments, for the word means apportion. "They parted my garments" - they gave one portion to each of the four soldiers. He had four garments, as I have said.

Then there was a fifth garment, called here His coat. "Now the coat was without seam, woven from the top throughout". Those are most suggestive words. We are going to examine them in detail. "They said therefore among themselves, Let us not rend it, but cast lots for it, whose it shall be: that the scripture might be fulfilled which saith" (we are back now in the great Psalm of the crucifixion, Psalm 22) "they parted my raiment among them, and for my vesture they did cast lots. These things therefore the soldiers did."

I want to build this message around five simple thoughts.

M---

Firstly, I want to examine the *Material* of the seamless robe.
Secondly, I want to examine the *Making* of the seamless robe.
Thirdly, I want to speak upon the *Meaning* of the seamless robe.
Fourthly, I want to underscore the *Message* of the seamless robe.
And last of all I want, for a little time, to consider the subject of all subjects - the *Mystery* of the seamless robe.

Brethren and sisters, we are on holy ground. We are on thrice holy ground. We are talking about something that carnal minds and unscriptural hearts do not understand. We have for our contemplation a wonderful subject. May God enliven our hearts, may God anoint our eyes with eye salve, may God so stir up our perception and conception of spiritual things, that in the hush of this assembly today we will see the making of the seamless robe which was made for the covering of ourselves, and the salvation of our souls.

## THE MATERIAL OF THE SEAMLESS ROBE

It is a well known fact that the inner robe of the Galilean peasant, in the time of our Lord, was made of linen. It was a linen robe. This, of course, corresponds with Revelation chapter nineteen. It says concerning the Church: "And to her was granted that she should be arrayed in fine linen, clean and white: for the fine linen is the righteousness of saints." But the saints of God had no righteousness of their own, the saints of God were only sinners, just as vile in their sins, just as hideous in their crimes as every other sinner in the world, but they are clothed in garments not their own. I would ask you to compare that scripture with 2 Corinthians chapter five and verse twenty. What is the righteousness of saints? What is this fine linen clean and white? Verse twenty-one of 2 Corinthians five: "For He hath made Him to be sin for us, who knew no sin; that we might be made the righteousness of God in Him". The righteousness of God in Him. The fact that this garment was made of linen is most significant.

Turn with me to the great book of the prophecy of Ezekiel. In this prophecy there is a very significant verse which is worthwhile underlining. It is the forty-fourth chapter and the verse eighteen. It has to do with the ministry of the priest, and what they should wear. It says, "And it shall come to pass, that when they enter in at the gates of the inner court, they shall be clothed with linen garments; and no wool shall come upon them, whiles they minister in the gates of the inner court and within. They shall have linen bonnets upon their heads, and shall have linen breeches upon their loins; they shall not gird themselves with anything that causeth sweat."

Just have a look at that carefully, every word is important. The priests in the Lord's house, as they ministered before the Lord in the temple were to be clothed with linen. And the reason given, they were not to gird themselves with wool or with any other garment which causes sweat. Of course the Bible is a wonderful book, it was not written by man, and if you study the scriptures you will find that only three times in the Word of God, does this word "sweat" occur.

If you go to Genesis 3:19, there "sweat" is first mentioned, and by the law of the first mention, which is a very important law in scripture, you will get the key to its meaning. (If you want to know what a thing symbolises in the Word of God, there is a great principle called the law of the first mention. Find out where it is first mentioned in the Word of God, and that gives you the key to open the whole doorway to an examination of that subject in the scriptures) Genesis chapter three and verse nineteen: "In the sweat of thy face". The curse on Adam! And sweat was the result of the curse, and typifies sin.

Only once in the New Testament does the word "sweat" occur, in Luke's Gospel chapter twenty-two and verse forty-four. Christ is in the garden of Gethsemane: "And being in an agony He prayed more earnestly: and His sweat was as it were great drops of blood falling down to the ground."

Do you get the significance? The first Adam sweat under the curse of sin. The last Adam sweat drops of blood to put away sin. But the priests in the temple were to be clothed with fine linen, so that the curse of the fall, "sweat", would not appear upon their garments. For the priests were to be characterised by holiness unto the Lord.

So the seamless robe is made of linen. There is no sweat upon it because it typifies the immaculate, impeccable, incorruptible, righteousness of Christ, righteousness which, praise His Holy Name, He has imputed to all that believe.

The Shorter Catechism states, "Justification is an act of God's free grace, wherein He pardoneth all our sins, and accepteth us as righteous in His sight. Only for the righteousness of Christ imputed to us, and received by faith alone."

And the day that God saved my sinful soul there was a great transaction. I was stripped of my rags of sin, and Jesus put upon me the fine linen robe, and I am going to wear it for all eternity. I got it at the Cross, and when I appear in glory with my Saviour, I will have on that linen robe for fine linen is the righteousness of saints.

So much for the material of the robe.

## THE MAKING OF THE SEAMLESS ROBE 2

We have a very significant mention in John nineteen. It is only in John's gospel that it occurs. This robe was without seam. It was not a patched-up garment, or a garment that was constructed by sewing pieces together. The righeousness of Christ is without seam. There are no joins in the righteousness of Christ. He did not live a righteous life for so long and then leave off. From the crib of Bethlehem to the cross of Calvary it is one right through, a seamless robe, not a seam within it and not a break throughout it. One precious thread, one precious life woven together into the perfect righteousness, for all that believe in Jesus.

Notice that it was woven from the top throughout. This garment, the inner garment, was a garment which was fastened around the neck, it had flowing sleeves, and it stretched right down to the feet and covered every member of the body. It commenced at the top, because Christ's body is a type of the church, and we are members of His body, and every member needs to be covered. This robe is not manufactured from the bottom to the top, because that would typify that our righteousness is something that we acquired or that we attained to. But righteousness is not an attainment but an obtainment, it is a gift. Hence it was woven from the top.

The head was not covered in this garment because Christ does not need any righteousness in and of Himself, because, as God, He is eternally righteous. The Lord Jesus Christ kept the law for you and me, and what the law could not do, in that it was weak through the flesh, God sent His own Son, in the likeness of sinful flesh, and for sin condemned sin in the flesh.

There was not a man from Adam onwards that could keep the law. Our garments are patched and stained. But the Blessed Son of God in His mediatorial capacity as the federal head of His church, dotted every "i" and stoked every "t" of the law. Before He entered upon His ministry, at His baptism, after living for thirty years, the span of a life, God could say, "This is My beloved Son, in whom I am well pleased." There was not one patch on His garment or seam in His life. It was absolutely perfect.

He lived in obscurity from the age of twelve to thirty. Why, what was He doing? I will tell you what He was doing. He was fulfilling God's law for you. I have heard preachers say that the life of Christ from twelve to thirty was unimportant. What utter nonsense! Ever minute Jesus lived was important, and from the age of twelve which, in the Jewish law, was the age of accountability, until the age of thirty when He entered upon His public ministry, he fulfilled God's law entirely. Yes and God looked down from heaven and said at His baptism, as He entered on His public ministry: "This is My beloved Son, in whom I am well pleased."

His garment was immaculate, it is woven from the top throughout. Praise God, it covers us all. We are unimportant members when we think of the more important members of the church. But praise God it covers right down to the feet. We are all included in the covering.

The making of the robe.

## THE MEANING OF THE ROBE

Let us look at the meaning of the robe. The garment in scripture denotes character. Turn over to the one hundred and ninth Psalm and you will find that. We have here a wicked man described, and it says in verse eighteen: "As he clothed himself with cursing like as with his garment". So the garment reflected his character. He was an evil man, and he clothed himself with cursing as with a garment. The righteous man is exhorted to clothe himself. Turn to I Peter chapter five and verse five: "Likewise, all of you be subject one to another, and be clothed with humility." So the garment speaks of character.

This robe of Christ was the most precious garment that He had. And when the soldiers saw it they realised that it was worth something. The other garments they were only the garments that all peasants had: the girdle, and the sandals and the headdress and the outer cloak. But here was this coat, and they looked upon it, and said, "Let us not rend it". If it had not been a rich garment those cruel men who nailed Him to the cross would have taken it and they would have rent it. But you know we read that there were women who ministered to the Lord. And I believe that those women that ministered to Him where those who made this garment for Him. This garment, as I have said, speaks to us of the righteousness of Christ. And I turn over to Galatians and I read this of my Saviour, "He was made of a woman, made under the law." The vehicle through which sin entered the world was the woman. Eve was first in sin. But God in His great wisdom said to the devil, "You have taken the woman to ruin the race but I will take her and make her the vehicle for the redemption of the race." And Christ was made of a woman, born of a virgin. It was women's hands that made this robe, I believe, and it was the woman's womb that God Almighty used for the incarnation of His precious Son. A costly garment!

We read that when the prodigal returned, the father said, "Bring the best robe and put it on him". That's what this garment means; it is the best robe; it is the righteousness of Christ; it is the robe of righteousness, it is the wedding garment Hallelujah! It permits us to sit down at the great marriage supper of the Lamb, and covers every member of the body.

## THE MESSAGE OF THE SEAMLESS ROBE

Let's look for a moment then at the message of the robe. It should be pointed out that this linen garment worn next to the flesh by the peasant was the same type of robe as was worn by the priest as an outer garment. It was worn by the general public as an inner garment but by the priest as an outer garment. Josephus in his Body of Jewish Antiquities points this out. The priest had this garment on the outside, the peasant had this garment on the inside. The Lord Jesus Christ upon the cross is our great high priest, and what did they do? They took off His garments, and just before His crucifying he was seen in the garment of the priest, for he was God's great high priest.

They then took that garment off Him. Why? Because He was made sin for you and me. He donned our rags and left us His robe. He took our sin, and He left us His righteousness. He was uncovered to God's wrath that we might be covered for all eternity from the wrath of a sin-hating God. That is why we sing "The wrath of a sin-hating God, with me can have nothing to do, my Saviour's obedience and blood hides all our transgressions from view." It hides! It covers! We are hidden! Where are we? We are in Christ, Hallelujah! And when God looks on us He sees not ourselves but the garment of His Son. We are like David. When David went into the presence of King Saul, he was clothed in the garments of Jonathan, the king's son, because Jonathan gave up his garments to David. And when I go into the presence of the King, I will be going there in the garments of Christ. Clothed in His garments! What a blessed message this is to the people of God.

You know there is something more about this. None of those four soldiers, by his own will, got that garment. The garment was disposed of by lot. Now go back to John nineteen, this is important: "They parted my garments among them, and for my vesture they did cast lots". Not one of those four could say, "That garment will be mine" No Sir. Because it was given by lot. Turn over to Proverbs sixteen and verse thirty-three: "The lot is cast into the lap; but the whole disposing thereof is of the Lord." So it is the Lord that controls the outcome of the lot. That is why, in the New Testament Church, they did not believe in the ballot for the electing of office bearers in the church. They cast lots.

In the early Puritan times office bearers in the church were appointed by the casting of lots. For the lot is presided over by the Lord. And the man who got Christ's garment at the cross was the man whom the Lord foreordained should get it. "The lot is cast into the lap; but the whole disposing thereof is of the Lord." And those that have got the righteousness of Christ did not get it by their own will or by their own choice, but they got it by sovereign grace alone.

"It is not of him that willeth, nor of him that runneth, but of God that sheweth mercy." I have faith today because God gave it. I was no better than anyone else and worse than many, but God in grace sent His gentle Spirit to my heart, convicted me of my sin, and while many of those that sat around me rejected God, yet through the triumph of grace I was enabled to close with Christ freely offered to me in the gospel. Today I have the righteousness of Christ. This is the message of this robe disposed of by my Lord.

## THE MYSTERY OF THE SEAMLESS ROBE

This robe has a mystery. Everything about Christ is mysterious. John talks about the vesture. He is the last one in the scriptures to write about the vesture. In Revelation he writes about it, for that vesture is seen in heaven. Let us turn to Revelation chapter nineteen. The Lord Jesus Christ is coming. The heaven is open. What a day that will be! Revelation chapter nineteen, verse eleven: "And I saw heaven opened, and behold a white horse; and he that sat upon him was called Faithful and True, and in righteousness he doth judge and make war." This is the triumphant Christ, Christ in His glorious advent. "His eyes were as a flame of fire, and on His head were many crowns; and He had a name written, that no man knew, but He Himself. And He was clothed (look at it) He was clothed with a vesture dipped in blood. Here is the vesture again in the glory. "And His name is called the Word of God". "And the armies which were in heaven followed Him upon white horses, clothed in fine linen, white and clean." I hope you are getting the connection.

He has a vesture dipped in blood, but those that followed Him are clothed in linen, white and clean. "And out of His mouth goeth a sharp sword, that with it He should smite nations: and He shall rule them with a rod of iron: and He treadeth the winepress of the fierceness and wrath of Almighty God. And He hath on His vesture (here is His vesture again) and on His thigh a name written, KING OF KINGS AND LORD OF LORDS."

The vesture at the advent. What a subject! Two things I want you to notice about it. This is a vesture dipped in blood, and this is a vesture on which there is inscribed a name. And those that come after Him are sharing in the covering of the vesture, because they have on fine linen, white and clean. What is the meaning of this? Very simple, Jesus Christ is coming again. But His second coming cannot be divorced from His first coming. Once in the end of the world has He appeared to put away sin, by the sacrifice of Himself. But to those that look for Him He shall appear a second time without sin, or apart from sin, unto salvation. But the strength of His second coming lies in the achievement of His first.

Jesus Christ shall wear a robe dipped in blood. He shall be followed by His saints, by His church, in garments white and clean. But these garments are also garments dipped in blood. For they sing, "Unto Him who loved us and washed us from our sins in His own blood." "Who are these arrayed in white robes? and whence came they? These are they that washed their robes in the blood of the Lamb." Jesus Christ in heaven wears the vesture dipped in blood. And every saint of God shall share in that blessed garment, that garment that summed up His whole sacrifice on the tree.

There is something else, this garment is now inscribed. "He has upon His vesture a name written, and also upon His thigh" Why is that? Go away back to old Jacob. You remember Jacob met with the angel at Peniel. He wrestled and as he wrestled God touched his thigh, and he went over the river with a limp, but he went over a prince with God. He is a type of Christ. My Saviour came to the great struggle of the cross, where He met the strong man. The prince of this world came and struggled with Christ. Thank God, Christ won the battle, but when He crossed the river, He bore the marks of His suffering with Him, right to heaven's glory. In other words, He went over with a limp, and on His thigh was written KING OF KINGS AND LORD OF LORDS. To old Jacob God said, "You are no longer Jacob. You are a prince, you have prevailed."

Praise God, my Saviour prevailed at Calvary. But not only upon His thigh, but upon His vesture it is written in the blood, that He is KING OF KINGS AND LORD OF LORDS.

I am not talking about Christ now as God the Son, in His capacity as co-equal with the Father. I am talking about Him now in His mediatorial capacity, when He took to His Deity our Humanity, and became the living Christ for our redemption.

God has highly exalted Him, and given Him a name that is above every name. And some day I will see my Saviour in the vesture of His sufferings. I will read in writing of precious blood, KING OF KINGS AND LORD OF LORDS.

Then shall every saint of God take up the palm of victory and strike the chords of the eternal Hallelujah chorus on the celestial harps of heaven, and the vaults of eternity will ring with the praises of my Saviour. What a day that will be when God's people read on His vesture: KING OF KINGS AND LORD OF LORDS. Thank God we have been cleansed in His blood, covered by His righteousness and it is well, praise God it is eternally well, with our souls.

# 4 The distinguished garments *of Christ*

**CONTINUED**

**I WANT TO CONTINUE** my message on a very precious subject "The Wardrobe of Christ". We have been looking, in the three previous messages, at the Garments of the Saviour. I said, at the outset of these particular messages on the garments of Christ, that we would deal first of all with "The Distinctive Garments of Christ".

First we had a message on the garments of Christ in their representative capacity, as signifying the Saviour's death. The first garment that pressed upon His baby form was the swaddling clothes of the shroud. He was born to die. We noticed also that the distinctive significance of His garments was the hem, the finished work. This signified His death for and on behalf of His people. The woman touched the hem of His garment and immediately she was made whole. We also saw that the crowds desired to touch the hem of His garment for in that finished work there is life over death and healing over every disease.

In our second message we looked at "The Distinguished Garments of Christ". We noted that they were five in number. In our third message we looked at the fifth garment, the vesture or the seamless robe.

Now we change our study slightly, and we come to look at "The Distinguished Garments of Christ" as He carries on His high priestly ministry.

I am turning to the first chapter of the book of the Revelation. "In the midst" (verse thirteen) "of the seven candlesticks one like unto the Son of man, clothed with a garment down to the foot, and girt about the paps with a golden girdle". Look at it, "clothed with a garment down to the foot, and girt about the paps with a golden girdle".

We saw in our first studies that the vesture or seamless robe of Christ, woven from the top throughout, without seam and without joins, was actually the distinguished garment of the priest which he wore on the outside. We discovered that this seamless robe of Christ was worn on the inside. The common people wore it on the inside. The seamless robe represented the Lord Jesus Christ in His priestly work.

If you turn to Matthew chapter twenty-seven, there is a very important passage there which must not be overlooked. (We will be coming to a more serious consideration of this thought, when we consider "The Discarded Garments of Christ").

Here in verse twenty-eight to thirty-two we have "The Discarded Garments of Christ". "They stripped Him and put on Him a scarlet robe. And when they had platted a crown of thorns, they put it upon His head, and a reed in His right hand: and they bowed the knee before Him, and mocked Him, saying, "Hail, King of the Jews!" And they spit upon Him, and they took the reed, and smote Him on the head. And after that they had mocked Him, they took the robe off from Him, and put His own raiment on Him". Mark it! The Lord Jesus Christ did not wear the scarlet robe, as He walked to Calvary. He wore the precious robes that were His own. Man has no part in the great sacrifice made for sins.

When He comes to Calvary, they take from off Him the coat. They take from off Him the girdle. They take from off Him the sandals. They take from off Him the headdress. Four garments in all. Before they nail him to the cross He stands in the seamless robe. The last garment that human eyes gazed upon before He was crucified was the priestly garment. Why? Because He is about to do the work of a priest and sacrifice Himself upon the cross. They took off that garment, the garment of the priest, and nailed Him to the tree.

The Lord Jesus Christ is now glorified. He is at God's right hand. He has a message for the beloved disciple John, the message of the Book of the Revelation. So on the Lord's Day the Lord Himself appears. May He appear to us on this His Day! There was a great trumpet sound. A great voice was heard. John turned around. What did He see in the midst of the seven candlesticks? "One like unto the Son of man, clothed" (mark that word) "clothed".

How was He clothed? He was clothed with "a garment down to the foot". This is the seamless robe again. Why? Because Jesus Christ is now doing for you and me the work of the great high priest. He is within the veil.

We saw Him before the cross and there He stands a priest before His fellows. Then He offers Himself a sacrifice for sins. Then, praise God, He puts on again the robe of the priest, and goes within the veil to present the efficacy of His precious blood, to do for you and me the work which the high priest did for the children of Israel.

Now we want to consider this garment: "the garment down to the foot". I have five things to say about this garment. All of them are worthy of careful study.

**A GARMENT OF IDENTIFICATION WITH HIS PEOPLE**

*He is identified with His people in the wearing of this garment.* Do you know that Aaron the high priest had garments that were peculiar to himself. No other priest wore these garments but the high priest. There was, of course, the ephod, the curious girdle, and the breastplate, garments peculiar to Aaron and to Aaron alone, and to the high priests which succeeded him.

All the priests, however, wore the linen garment down to the foot. It was a garment common to them all. Turn to Exodus chapter thirty-nine, and you can confirm that. "And they made coats of fine linen" (verse twenty-seven) "of woven work for Aaron, and for his sons. And a mitre of fine linen, and goodly bonnets of fine linen, and linen breeches of fine twined linen. And a girdle of fine twined linen, and blue, and purple, and scarlet, of needlework as the Lord commanded Moses".

I want you to notice that the coats of fine linen were not only for Aaron but also for his sons. Turn over to Leviticus chapter eight verses six and seven, "And Moses brought Aaron and his sons, and washed them with water. And he put upon him the coat, and girded him with the girdle, and clothed him with the robe, and put the ephod upon him, and he girded him with the curious girdle of the ephod, and bound it unto him herewith. And he put the breastplate upon him: also he put in the breastplate the Urim and the Thummin. And he put the mitre upon his head; also upon the mitre, even upon his forefront, did he put the golden plate, the holy crown; as the Lord commanded Moses". Look at verse thirteen; "And Moses brought Aaron's sons, and put coats upon them; as the Lord commanded Moses". So the one garment which was common to all the priests was this particular garment. The Lord Jesus Christ wears this garment of the priest. You will notice moreover that this garment has also upon it a crown. The high priest was not only a priest, but he was a king. Now the Lord Jesus Christ is the great king priest of His people. Turn to Revelation chapter one and verse six, and you will find that the Lord Jesus Christ has identified us, not only with His priesthood but with His kingship "He has made us kings and priests unto God and His Father". The garment is the garment of identification with His people. When He wears that garment, He identifies Himself with us.

I want you to notice in Revelation chapter one, four ways in which the Lord Jesus Christ is identified with His people. When the voice was heard John turned around and saw seven golden candlesticks, and Jesus in the midst of those candlesticks.

*He is identified with His people in relationship to the church*. Those candlesticks represent the church. The Lord Jesus Christ is closely identified with His church,. He is the great King and He is the Head of the church.

He is not only identified with His people in the church. Look at it "One like unto the Son of *God*". It does not say that. Mark it carefully. For the Lord Jesus Christ is identified with His people in His title: "One like unto the Son of *man". He is identified with humanity here, with all the sinful sons of men, who are His own, redeemed with precious blood.*

He is identified with the church.

He is identified with humanity.

Thirdly, He is *identified with every minister of the church*. In His hand He has seven stars, and those stars are the angels of the Church.

When I was a boy I wondered where the angel was in the church. I knew that some women folk claimed to be angels, although they did not act like it in the church. I knew that! When I grew older I learned that the angel is the messenger, the angelos, the minister. For every church there is one minister, and that minister is held in the hand of Christ. Hallelujah!

The minister is not upheld by the Church Committee or the Kirk Session, or the Presbytery, or the General Assembly. He is upheld by the nail-pierced hand of Christ.

Fourthly, *He is identified with every member of His body because He is clothed with this garment down to the foot*. His foot is mentioned later on. This is very important. We must study it carefully. You see His garment is mentioned first. Then His head which is not covered with the garment is mentioned. Look at it: "His head and His hairs were white like wool, as white as snow; And His feet like unto fine brass, as if they burned in a furnace;"

Now there are two important things here. Very important! There are the similes. What are His head and hairs like? "His head and His hairs are like wool, as white as snow". Now those two similes are only used in the Bible of one other thing. Turn over with me to Isaiah chapter one, verse eighteen, "Come now, and let us reason together, saith the Lord: though your sins be as scarlet, they shall be as white as snow; though they be red like crimson, they shall be as wool". There you have the two similes again, "snow and wool".

There is a deep significance of course in those two similes in regard to God's people. Snow has a whiteness which man cannot manufacture because it comes from heaven. Wool is produced by life. The deep significance is that the Lord Jesus Christ was led as "a lamb to the slaughter" but "as a sheep before her shearers is dumb". You will notice the change. He is the lamb for the slaughter but He is the sheep for the shearing. There would not be enough wool on the lamb to cover us, and the lamb would not be a full life. It would only be the life born.

The sheep represents the whole life, the sum total of living. Praise God, the sum total of Christ's life, in all His thirty-three years of perfection on earth, dotting every "i" and stroking every "t" of God's law, was poured out in the blood of the Lamb, and becomes a perfect covering for all my sins. Those are the two similes here used in connection with Christ.

Turn to the Song of Solomon. There is a vision of the Lord in the Song of Solomon. If you look carefully at that vision, you will discover that the Lord's hair is not white in that vision. Solomon's Song chapter five, verse eleven, "His head is as the most fine gold, His locks are bushy, and black as a raven". When we come to the New Testament, however, His head and His hairs are white like snow, as white as wool. Why? Because between Solomon's Song and the book of Revelation there stands the cross.

Jesus Christ has gone into the fire. Jesus Christ has borne all the torments of judgment. He now stands with the marks of suffering upon Him. "His head and His hairs were white like wool, as white as snow".

Further, look at it, "His feet like unto fine brass, as if they burned in a furnace". There is judgment again. Brass in scripture always speaks of judgment. Silver in scripture always speaks of redemption. That is why the pillars in the tabernacle were set in sockets of silver, for the actual construction of the holy place and the holiest of all. They typify Christ's people in the church who stand on the ground of redemption. The poles which made up the outer court in the tabernacle were set in sockets of brass. They typify the Christian out in the world. The world does not understand our standing on the ground of redemption. Our testimony to the world is that judgment is beneath our feet, so the sockets of brass typify the believer in relationship to the world.

Now Christ's feet are like brass burning in the furnace. Do you know that the first part of the body of Christ ever mentioned in the scripture is His feet. The great gospel promise "He shall bruise thy head, thou shall bruise His heel". The first part of the Lord's body ever mentioned in scripture is His heel.

Now if you want a very interesting and helpful study, study the feet of the Lord Jesus Christ. The feet that were washed with the woman's tears and wiped with the hairs of her head; the first part of the Lord's body which ever was touched after He rose from the dead was His feet; the woman clasped His feet and the feet of Jesus were bruised by the serpent. Now do you get it? Between His head and His feet there is worked out a perfect robe of covering. This is the message of this robe which stretches from His head to His feet. It is a robe of identification with His people. He is identified with you and me. Every member of His mystical body is covered.

What does He say in Revelation three and verse four: "Thou hast a few names even in Sardis which have not defiled their garments; and they shall walk with me in white for they are worthy". You identify yourself with the people with whom you walk. The Lord Jesus Christ has put on the robe of identification with His people and those who walk with Him shall "walk in white, for they are worthy".

## A GARMENT OF EXALTATION TO HIS PEOPLE

It is the garment of rest. There is one difference between this garment and the garment of the high priest. The garment of the high priest has the girdle around the loins. This garment has the girdle around the breast.

When the girdle is around the loins it means the work has still to be done. "Gird up the loins of your mind, be strong and hope to the end" is an exhortation to work. Elijah girded up his loins, and ran before the chariot of Ahab. When work has to be done, the girdle is at the loins. But, praise God, Jesus has finished the work, and the girdle is now over His heart. Love takes the place of service, and affection takes the place of work. We are identified with this garment in our rest, our work is done. Turn to Revelation chapter six and verse nine: "And when He had opened the fifth seal, I saw under the altar the souls of them that were slain for the Word of God, and for the testimony which they held. And they cried with a loud voice saying, How long, O Lord, holy and true, dost thou not judge and avenge our blood on them that dwell on the earth? And white robes were given unto every one of them; and it was said unto them; that they should rest". Mark it! "Rest". The robe indicates the resting. Hallelujah!

My Saviour has rested from His labours. No longer is the girdle at His loins but the girdle is at His breast. It is a girdle of pure gold, speaking of the fact that His priestly work is now superseded by His kingly dominion. For my Saviour is coming again, not as a priest, but He is coming again as my King, "LORD OF LORDS, AND KING OF KINGS".

The garment speaks of identification with His people, but it also speaks of exaltation to His people. May the Lord stir our hearts, and may we remember that His garments smell of aloes, cassia, myrrh. Yes and may each one of us love Him with all our hearts.

# 5 The distinguished garments *of Christ*

**CONTINUED**

**I WANT TO CONTINUE** our studies in "The Wardrobe of Christ" or the Garments of our blessed Saviour. If you turn back in your Bible to the sixty-third chapter of Isaiah you read this most suggestive description of the garments of Christ. "Who is this that cometh from Edom, with dyed garments from Bozrah? this that is glorious in His apparel". We have been looking at the glorious apparel of the Lord Jesus Christ.

We looked in our first meditation upon "The Distinctive Garments of Christ". We noticed that His garments were characterised by death in the estate of His humiliation when He was upon this earth.

The first garment that pressed His baby body was the wrapping of the shroud, "She wrapped Him in swaddling clothes". He was born to die.

We also saw that the distinctive garment which He wore, as He walked life's pilgrimage, was the garment with the hem. The hem is the finished work. The woman said: "If I could but touch the hem of His garment, I shall be made whole". And it is in the death of Christ alone that healing and succour and salvation come.

In the second place we viewed "The Distinguished Garments of Christ". We had a look at the five garments which the Saviour wore, when He walked this scene of time. We had a look at the headdress. We had a look at the sandals. We had a look at the girdle. We had a look at the outer garment and we had a look at the seamless robe, the most interesting, the most instructive and the most precious of all His garments. It is the garment of the priest, the garment worn next to the flesh. It is the priestly robe, the seamless garment.

Having looked at those garments, we have now come to the Book of Revelation. We are now considering the garments which He wears in heaven. In the first chapter of Revelation we have a vision of our glorified Lord. John saw Him. Verse thirteen of Revelation chapter one; "And in the midst of the seven candlesticks one like unto the Son of man, clothed with a garment down to the foot, and girt about the paps with a golden girdle", We have already looked at this garment of Christ. We have noticed that this is the same seamless robe. It is the same priestly garment. It is now the garment of the priest within the veil.

You know the garments of glory and beauty which the high priest wore were not worn on the day of atonement. They were worn for all the services of the tabernacle and temple but on the day of atonement he wore only one garment, this garment of fine linen. The linen garment was worn alone on the day of atonement.

Christ, of course, has gone within the veil and there He sits in our stead today. He wears this priestly garment, the anti-type of the linen garment worn by the high priest when he ministered within the veil.

We noticed that this garment was a garment of *Identification with His people*. That was the first point we dealt with. We noticed some things: He is identified with His people as He wears this garment. He is called (look at it carefully) not the Son of *God*, but the Son of *man*. Of course He is the Son of God and He is the God the Son. By identification with His people, He takes the humble title, Son of man. This thus identifies Himself with our humanity. "We have not an high priest that cannot be touched with the feelings of our infirmities". We have a sympathising High priest. There is not a pain which rends the human heart, but the Man of Sorrows hath a part. He is identified with us in His name. He is identified with us in His place, "and in the midst of the seven candlesticks". The seven candlesticks are the church, and the Lord Jesus is identified with His church.

You remember Paul persecuted the church. The Lord Jesus Christ felt it in heaven. He said to Saul, "Saul, Saul, why persecutest thou me". Matthew Henry comments: "When the foot was bruised on earth, the Head cried out in heaven". Oh, it is true! And when the church is bruised on earth, the Lord Jesus Christ feels it in heaven. He is identified with us. My dear believer, whatever problem you have, Jesus understands. But it is one thing to understand a person's problem and another thing to feel for them. But my Saviour feels as well. His understanding is the understanding of the great sympathiser, of the great consoler, of the great succourer of His people.

Then we saw the Lord Jesus Christ identified with HIs people in two other things. In His description, verse fourteen, "His head and His hairs were white like wool, as white as snow". I pointed out that the simile is only used in one other place in scripture. It is used of the cleansing of the people of God. "Though your sins be as scarlet, they shall be as white as snow; though they be red like crimson they shall be as wool". So His head speaks to us of His pardoning love.

"His feet like unto fine brass, as if they burned in a furnace". The first part of the body of Christ ever mentioned in scripture is His foot. "He shall bruise thy head, but thou shalt bruise his heel". This speaks of the cross. For the members of His body are in between the head and the feet of Jesus, in this long covering robe. Thus He identifies Himself with His people. I dealt with that fully, but I must repeat it so that we can follow the sequence of the message.

The second thing I pointed out previously is that this is the garment of *Exaltation with His people*.

Turn over to Revelation chapter nineteen, and it says there that Christ was "clothed with a vesture dipped in blood". "For my vesture did they cast lots". It is the same priestly garment. But look at it. "And the armies which were in heaven followed Him upon white horses, clothed in fine line, white and clean". They are identified with His garment in the glory.

The high priest had a garment of fine twined linen which he wore next to his body, in the privacy, covered over with other garments. The other priests had only one garment and it was the outer garment to them. The righteousness of Christ is a secret thing, wrought out for us in the silence of those years called "the silent years" in His ministry. But we who have been made kings and priests unto God, wear this garment outwardly because it makes us acceptable to God in Jesus Christ, and one day we will wear it eternally, in the day of our exaltation.

I want to show you that this garment is not only the garment of *Identification with His people,* and of *Exaltation along with His people,* but

**IT IS THE GARMENT OF PROPITIATION FOR HIS PEOPLE**

"The soul that sinneth it shall die". "No man can see God and live". In the presence of God, sinners die. Need I emphasise? I think I would need to emphasise that death in the scripture is never annihilation, it is always separation. The person that dies is in a state of separation. Physical death is the separation of the spiritual part of the body from the material part. That is quite simple. Eternal death is the eternal separation of the physical and spiritual part of man eternally from God in the lake of fire. "The soul that sinneth it shall die."

Now look at the first chapter of Revelation. You will notice what John saw: "In the midst of the golden candlesticks one like unto the Son of man clothed with a garment down to the foot". But at the end of his vision, he had got his eye off the garment. "His countenance was as the sun shineth in his strength". Immediately the eye of John was taken off the garment which speaks of propitiation for His people what happened? He fell at His feet as dead. No man can see God and live. The priest was told that if he did not wear the garment he would die.

You will remember the man who came into the wedding feast. The master of the feast said "Friend, why hast thou not on the wedding garment? And he was taken out and his portion was death".

Now let us look at it. When John fell at His feet as dead, the Lord Who had on the garment, put His right hand on John. It was a nail-pierced hand which He put on him, and He said, "Fear not". He then emphasised three things. Number one, He emphasised *His Person*: "I am the First and the Last". Number two, He emphasised *His Passion*, in the very descriptive words, "I am He that liveth, and was dead, And behold, I am alive". In those words you have the whole passion of Christ. His sacrifice summed up. He was the One Who lived. He was the One Who died in propitiation for our sins, and He is the One Who lives again. Number three, He emphasised *His Power* "And have the keys of hell and of death". The One Who wears the robes holds the keys. He is the propitiation for our sins. And He will never lock a child of His into hell and death. He has got the key!

I was in the prison this morning and coming out I was glad that the warder had the keys or I would still have been there. I got out, but there were about fifty fellows at the service I conducted who would love to have come out with me. They were not permitted. The warder had the orders to open the door for me only. The Lord Jesus Christ has opened the door of death and hell for His people and He has closed that door and locked it eternally against us. He wears the robe, the garment of propitiation for us, and if you keep your eye upon the One Who is clothed with that garment you will rejoice with joy unspeakable and full of glory. "He that hath the Son hath life".

I want now to come further into this subject. It is not only the garment of our *Identification with Him*. It is not only the garment of our *Exaltation along with Him*. It is not only the garment of *Propitiation for His people,* but I will say something more.

## IT IS THE GARMENT OF IMPUTATION UPON HIS PEOPLE

Now turn back with me to Exodus chapter thirty-nine and verses twenty-seven, or perhaps we might look first of all at Exodus chapter twenty-eight and verse thirty-nine: "And thou shalt embroider the coat of fine linen". This is the coat of the High priest. "And thou shalt make the mitre of fine linen, and thou shalt make the girdle of needlework".

"Thou shalt embroider the coat of fine linen". Turn over in the same book to chapter thirty-nine and verse twenty-seven: "And they made coats of fine linen of woven work for Aaron, and for his sons". Now turn over to Leviticus chapter eight, where we see these garments put on. (These are very important scriptures in our meditation, and I trust you will note them carefully, as we will be coming back to them as we continue our studies). Leviticus chapter eight and verses six and seven: And Moses brought Aaron and his sons and washed them with water. And he put upon him the coat and girded him with the girdle, and clothed him with the robe, and put the ephod upon him". You will notice the first thing that he put upon him was the coat. That is the garment which we are discussing at the moment. That was the first thing which was put upon him. You will notice that he not only clothed Aaron but he also clothed the priests, after they were washed.

Notice that there was *a difference between the coats of the ordinary priests and the coat of the high priest*. The coat of the high priest was an embroidered coat, like our damask, into its weaving went the design. The design was not imprinted upon it, it was part of its texture. There is a difference between our righteousness and the righteousness of the Saviour. The righteousness of the Saviour was part of His Person. It is interwoven into His life. It is something inherent to His whole character and to His whole experience. But the righteousness which we have is a righteousness imputed to us. Hence the difference in the type, the Holy Ghost makes this abundantly clear.

The ordinary priest had fine linen garments, but the high priest had the embroidered garment. The righteousness of Christ which He gives us is something absolutely inherent to Himself. It is imputed to us and received by faith alone.

The second thing I want you to notice, *the high priest was washed before the garment was placed on him, as were the other priests.*

But not so with the Lord Jesus Christ. He needed no cleansing before He put on this beautiful garment. If you turn over with me to Hebrews, you have a beautiful comment on the Lord's character there. The Epistle to the Hebrews chapter seven and verse twenty-four "But this man, because He continueth ever, hath an unchangeable priesthood. Wherefore He is able to save them to the uttermost that come unto God by Him, seeing He ever liveth to make intercession for them". "For such an high priest became us, who is holy, harmless, undefiled, separate from sinners, and made higher than the heavens".

(1) He is holy. (2) He is harmless. (3) He is undefiled. (4) He is separate from sinners. (5) He is made higher than the heavens. Five things. Five in scripture is the number of grace, and the righteousness of Christ is imputed to us by grace alone. We do not deserve it. I deserve judgment and hell. Praise God, I will never burn in hell because I have on the garment of His righteousness. "Jesus Thy blood and righteousness, My beauty are, my glorious dress, Midst flaming worlds in these arrayed, With joy will I lift up my head."

Now when you are studying the scriptures you should always watch the words. The last time "clothed" in the Bible is used, it is used in verse thirteen in Revelation chapter nineteen. Let us look at it, it is very important. It is used of Christ. It is the last time the word "clothed" is used in the scriptures. "And he was clothed in a vesture dipped in blood". The first time the word "clothed" was mentioned in the Bible is in the third chapter of Genesis. Very important. And in the third chapter of Genesis we read this: "Unto Adam also, and to his wife did the Lord make coats of skins and clothed them". I want you to notice that. We have a symbolism here, and we have a symbolism of deep significance.

The vesture which clothes Christ is the vesture of His high priestly work, which is imputed to us. It is the vesture of righteousness. Revelation nineteen verse eight: "And to her was granted that she should be arrayed in fine linen, clean and white; for the fine linen is the righteousness of saints". Adam and Eve had sinned. They tried to cover themselves, not clothe themselves, for man cannot clothe himself. They made fig leaf aprons. If you turn with me to the twenty-first verse of Genesis chapter three you will read "Unto Adam also and to his wife did the Lord God make coats of skins". I was looking at that verse in the Hebrew, and I noted that the word "skins" is not in the plural, it is in the singular. The Lord God made coats of skin. That means there was only one sacrifice, only one. He did not kill many animals, but the skin that covered Adam, and the skin that covered Eve came from the one sacrifice. Now there is only one sacrifice for sins for ever. Hallelujah! That makes every sacrificing priest redundant. I declare them all on the Unemployment Exchange. Let me tell you this, there is only one sacrifice.

Of course, man did not write the Bible. If man had written the Bible he would have said "coats of skins". It would have been all right. But it is coats of skin. What does that mean? There was ample to cover Adam. There was ample to cover Eve. Yes, and praise God, in the one sacrifice for sins forever there is a covering for all who will trust in the blood of the Lamb. The word "cover" or "clothe" is an interesting word in the Hebrew. It is the word from which we get "atonement". The very same word. It is the same word that is used of the Ark. Do you remember the Ark was pitched with pitch within and without. It was covered within and without. What does that mean? When God looked down from heaven, He saw the covering, the word from which we get "atonement". And when Noah sat inside the Ark and looked up, he saw the pitch. What does it mean? It means that God sees Christ, and I see Christ, and I am safe, Hallelujah! for evermore.

If we could only see Him in this garment, we could sing with all the elect the songs of heaven Unto Him Who loved us and washed us from our sins, in His own blood". As the ordinary priests were washed before they put on the garment so before I can put on the garment of Christ's righteousness, I must wash at the fountain filled with blood. And having washed in that fountain, I am clothed with the righteousness of Christ.

## THIS IS THE GARMENT OF REPRESENTATION ON BEHALF OF HIS PEOPLE

Jesus Christ stands within the veil. I want you to notice that the girdle is not about His loins. When a man has a girdle about his loins in scripture he is going out to work. The girdle is about His breast, because His work is all finished. That girdle is a breastplate, and the high priest carried the names of the tribes of Israel in two places upon his robes. He carried them upon his shoulders: "for the

Government is upon the shoulder". He also carried them on the golden breast-plate. It was over his heart.

My dear believer, there is a golden girdle around His heart today, for He carries our names right now in His work of intercession.

"My name from the palms of His hands, Eternity will not erase, Impressed on His heart it remains, In marks of indelible grace. Yes I to the end shall endure, As sure as the earnest is given, More happy, but not more secure, When glorified with Him in Heaven."

Let us look upon our blessed Lord, and as we see Him let us remember He wears the garment of *identification with us,* He wears the garment of *exaltation along with us*, He wears the garment of *propitiation for us*, and Praise God, He wears the garment of *representation on our behalf.*

# 6 The distinguished garments *of Christ*

**CONTINUED**

**TURN TO THE SIXTY-THIRD** chapter of Isaiah.

I want to continue this special series of messages on "The Wardrobe of Christ" or the Garments of our blessed Lord.

In our first study we looked at The Distinctive Garments of Christ, garments that were distinctive of the Lord's goal, the Lord's objective, the Lord's purpose, His sacrificial death.

They wrapped Him in a shroud when He was born. Swaddling clothes are typical of death. All His life He wore the garment with the hem upon it, the hem being the finished work, and those that touched the hem of His garment instantly were made whole.

We passed on to consider The Distinguished Garments of Christ. We looked at the five garments which the Saviour wore; the headdress, the sandals, the outer coat, the girdle, and the inner vestment. We spent some considerable time considering that vestment, the most important garment of them all.

We had also a look at the garment which He wears now in Revelation chapter one. "He is clothed with a garment down to the foot". We noticed that the first mention of the word "clothed" was the clothing of Adam and Eve - not in coats of skins (plural) but in coats of skin (singular). One sacrifice fully covered them both.

We considered some other wonderful things about that garment. His girdle is no longer around His loins because His work is done, but around His breast because He keeps the names of His people upon His heart. A wonderful Saviour. My Lord has garments that are wondrous rare.

## THE QUESTION ASKED AND ANSWERED

I want to finish this section of our studies on The Distinguished Garments of Christ by comparing two scriptures. The first is found in Isaiah sixty-three "Who is this that cometh from Edom, with dyed garments from Bozrah? This that is glorious in his apparel, travelling in the greatness of his strength?" There is the question, and then we have the answer. The Lord Himself answers the question "I that speak in righteousness, mighty to save. Wherefore art thou red in thine apparel, and thy garments like him that treadeth in the winefat? I have trodden the winepress alone; and of the people there was none with me; for I will tread them in mine anger, and trample them in my fury; and their blood shall be sprinkled upon my garments, and I will stain all my raiment."

You know we often lose the meaning of passages of scripture by considering only the particular chapter in which we find them. There were no chapters when the books of the Old Testament were originally written. There were no verses when the books of the Old and New Testament were originally written. The verses and the chapters were made by man to help Bible students when they handle a concordance to find out where the passages are.

You need to go back to chapter sixty-two verse eleven, to get the connection of the first verses of sixty-three: "Behold, the Lord hath proclaimed unto the end of the world say ye to the daughter of Zion, Behold, thy salvation cometh! 'Who is he that cometh from Bozrah' 'Behold, thy salvation cometh: behold, his reward is with him, and his work before him. And they shall call them, The holy people, The redeemed of the Lord: and thou shalt be called, Sought out, A city not forsaken'. Who is this that cometh from Edom?" If you pay particular attention to the connection you will find that the whole scripture will open up to you in a most luminous manner.

Now this scripture must be compared to the scripture which we read in Revelation chapter nineteen. Now keep your finger in chapter sixty-three of Isaiah and turn over to Revelation chapter nineteen, and in chapter nineteen you will find the fulfilment of the prophetic import of the scripture in Isaiah sixty-three. We looked at verse eleven of Revelation chapter nineteen: "And I saw heaven opened, and behold a white horse: and he that sat upon him was called Faithful and True, and in righteousness he doth judge and make war". "And he had on his vesture and on his thigh a name written, KING OF KINGS, AND LORD OF LORDS". Verse thirteen: "And he was clothed with a vesture dipped in blood: and His name is called The Word of God".

If you go down a little further in the chapter you will find that there is something said concerning the Lord which is very important indeed. Verse fifteen. "And he treadeth the winepress of the fierceness and wrath of Almighty God". Compare this with verse three of Isaiah sixty-three "I have trodden the winepress alone". And then at the end of the chapter you have the second supper (Revelation nineteen verse seventeen).

There are two suppers in this chapter of God's Word. Look at verse seven "Let us be glad and rejoice , and give honour to him; for the marriage of the Lamb is come, and his wife hath made herself ready". Verse nine, "Blessed are they which are called unto the marriage *supper* of the Lamb". Then if you go down to verse seventeen you have: "Come and gather yourselves together unto the *supper* of the great God". There is a great difference between these suppers. One is the supper of glorification, and the other is the supper of damnation. One speaks of heaven and the other speaks of hell.

The Lord Jesus Christ at the cross of Calvary not only did a delivering work, but He also did a destructive work. "He destroyed him that had the power of death, that is to say the devil" Hebrews two verses fourteen and fifteen. That is the destructive work. "And delivered them that through fear of death were all their lifetime subject to bondage." That is the deliverance work. One,

Destruction. Two, Deliverance. We will not realise the real teaching of these two portions of scripture until we get these things clearly before us.

Now let us go back to the sixty-third chapter of Isaiah and have a look at these garments. These two passages, Isaiah sixty-three and Revelation nineteen, refer to both the first and the second advents of Christ. Of course Revelation nineteen refers solely to the second advent of Christ. But in Isaiah sixty-three you have a reference to both the first and second advents.

Christ is pictured in this portion of scripture not only destroying His enemies but delivering His people. The main burden of the passage is salvation. Turn over to Isaiah sixty-two and verse eleven: "Say ye to the daughter of Zion, Behold, thy salvation cometh". And then turn to the answer in chapter sixty-three and verse one: "I that speak in righteousness, mighty to save". So the burden of these passages is salvation.

There is special emphasis placed upon the garments, and the garments are described with that wonderful expression "glorious in his apparel". I want to give you five reasons why the Lord Jesus Christ's garments are described as glorious.

## 1. THE APPAREL IS GLORIOUS BECAUSE OF ITS WEARER

The garment is glorious because of its wearer. The prophet has heard the triumphant marching feet of the great captain of his salvation. He has had a vision, a vision of the mighty conqueror. As he stands and views the Saviour he asks a question "Who is this?" "Who is this?" That question has four characteristics.

### *Firstly, it is a note of inquiry*

You see the soul is burdened. Sin has become unbearable. The awful load of our transgressions has pressed upon our heart, and then we know the gospel as it is echoed in verse eleven of Isaiah sixty-two "Behold, the Lord hath proclaimed unto the end of the world, Say ye to the daughter of Zion, Behold, thy salvation cometh; behold, his reward is with him, and his work before him". When the sinner has learned the burden of his sin and the corruption of his own evil heart, and feels the pangs that conviction of sin brings to him, immediately he inquires after the Saviour and exclaims "Who is this?" Can the Saviour really save me? Can my burden really be lifted? Can my blinded eyes really be opened? Can I really pass form death to life and from the power of sin and Satan unto God? And the answer is "I that speak in righteousness, mighty to save".

A dear lady came into the Kirk Session room last Sabbath night deeply burdened with a heart problem and a soul problem. Thank God she met the One who is able to save, and the burden was lifted and the sorrow was assuaged by the consolation of the gospel.

So the first thing is this, it is a note of inquiry when we ask this question "Who is this?"

*Secondly, it is an echo of ignorance*

We do not know who He is. The apostle Paul worked for Christ for twenty-five years and at the end of the day he said "that I might know Him". Alas, we do not know Him the way we should. No one knew the Saviour better than Mary Magdalene. Oh, she had been cleansed by the Saviour's Word of power and out of her heart seven demons had been cast. Yet one day, standing weeping at the sepulchre of the Master, Jesus drew near and she did not know Him. "Supposing Him to be the gardener".

Sometimes as we stand at the sepulchre of life's hopes, with tears running down our cheeks, Jesus comes and talks to us and we do not know Him. We suppose He is someone else. There is an echo of ignorance here. "Who is this?"

Two men who walked with Jesus for many a long day, one day went walking along the road to Emmaus. A stranger came and joined Himself to their company. As they walked along He expounded to them the scriptures, but they did not know Him although they had been with Him for years.

Many a time we have walked life's journey and Jesus has drawn near, and He has gone with us and we did not know Him. There is an echo of ignorance here.

You remember one day Peter said "I go afishing" and the other disciples went with him, and One stood upon the shore and said, "Children, have you any meat?" and they did not know Him. They thought He was a stranger. So in this question there is the echo of ignorance "Who is this?" Praise God, it is the Lord. It is the Lord!

Right beside you at the sepulchre where you have buried your hopes, not the gardener, but Jesus stands. Along that road which you walked with heavy heart, Jesus was with you., Oh, that you might see Him in the glory of His apparel. That glory is the glory if its wearer.

*Thirdly, it is a mark of amazement*

The old prophet is amazed, and he cries out: "Who is this that has succeeded in carrying the ramparts of Bozrah, and defeating the ancient enemies of Israel, the Edomites? Who is He?"

And so today we cry out with amazement as we ponder this chapter, Revelation nineteen. "I saw the heavens opened". Praise God, some day we shall see heaven opened. And one day every dot of every "i" and every stroke of every "t" in this chapter will be literally fulfilled. We shall see Him and shall we not say "Who is this?" It is a mark of amazement.

The last thing there is in this question is *a cry of adoration*.

"Who is this?" And if you note now the scripture goes "That this is glorious in His apparel" "Who is this?" "This that is glorious in His apparel".

So the first thing I want to say is the apparel is glorious because of its wearer.

## 2. THE APPAREL IS GLORIOUS BECAUSE OF ITS MESSAGE

Christ has put on says the Bible the "garments of salvation". I want you to look with me now at those last two verses in Isaiah chapter sixty-two, and you will find there are five things about salvation.

*Number one. It is external*

It is not something from inside you which regenerates you. It is someone from outside you who regenerates you. Look at it, it says: "Behold, thy salvation cometh". And then look at verse twelve "Sought out". There, my friend, you have the grace of God.

That garment has a message and its message is a message of external salvation. We are not saved from the inside but from the outside.

We are not saved by anything inherent within us, we are saved by something that comes into us from heaven. The blessed Holy Ghost does the work. The Spirit answers to the blood that I am born of God. "Thy salvation cometh.

God grant that a wave of salvation will come to Ulster at this time, that the mighty grace of God will triumph over the blight and the pollution of men, and we will see this gospel riding majestically in all its conquering and overcoming power.

*The second thing about this salvation, it is through a Person*

"Behold, the Lord hath proclaimed unto the end of the world, Say ye to the daughter of Zion, Behold, thy salvation cometh". "Behold, (mark it) His reward is with Him, and His work before Him". It is salvation through a Person. Yes!

We are not saved by creed. We are not saved by sacraments. We are not saved by ordinances. We are not saved by any system of men. Salvation is vested in the Person of the Saviour.

*The third thing about salvation, it is a salvation which redeems*

Look at it: "The redeemed of the Lord". What does redeem mean? Redeem means "buying back". It is the idea of the slave market, and the bidding is on. Thank God there is a great bidder Who comes into the slave market and He presents for our redemption the Blood of Himself. That blood has paid our debt, divine justice is satisfied because Christ is crucified, and the devil is terrified for I am justified. That is good! Praise God for it. What a wonderful thing to be redeemed.

*Fourthly, this salvation is a salvation which purifies*

Any other salvation is a farce, friend. You show me a man who says he is saved and is living persistently in sin, and I will show you a liar. Show me a man who says he is born again and he does the same things as the worldling, and I will show you a man who never knew the grace of God. What does it say? It says here "the holy people" praise God!

When God saves a man He finishes his past. The old things are finished, Hallelujah! and all things become new. This is real salvation.

*Fifthly, this salvation is an eternal salvation.*

How do I know that? "A city not forsaken". And praise God He will never forsake those who are washed in the Blood of the Lamb.

Five things about this salvation. That is the message of the glorious garment. This garment, this apparel is glorious because of its message.

But let me come to a sweeter thought even than that.

## 3. THIS APPAREL IS GLORIOUS BECAUSE OF ITS STAINS

It is a stained garment. "Wherefore art thou red in thine apparel".

Jesus Christ shed the blood of His foes by the shedding of His own Blood.

I was reading a little book by Samuel Rutherford the other day, "Sacramental Addresses" given at Anworth by Solway. Last year we went and visited that little church. It would have held, I suppose, a hundred people. There the saintly Samuel Rutherford ministered. The enemies of truth put him in prison. Samuel Rutherford says in one of those sermons. "I love my Saviour, but I love Him best of all when He is bonny red". "When He is bonny red".

The Lord Jesus Christ looks His best in the crimson vest of His suffering. At the cross when every other garment was taken from Him He clothed Himself in His own most precious Blood.

He put on these garments in order to redeem us, and the stains that are in His garments are indelible stains. They never wear or wash out. They are there forever.

When He comes again the marks of His sufferings will still be upon Him. Thank God. Those wounds still visible above will be visible for all eternity. Your redeemed body will not have a flaw or a spot or wrinkle. The body of Christ will bear the marks of His sufferings on the cross for all eternity. Yes, I like Him best as the Lamb newly slain in the midst of the Throne. The Lamb is all the glory in Emmanuel's land. The apparel is glorious because of its stains.

## 4. THE APPAREL IS GLORIOUS BECAUSE OF ITS ENDURANCE

Oh yes! this garment has come a long way and endured a long time.

Now let us get back to Isaiah chapter sixty-three. It says: "Who is this that cometh from Edom, with dyed garments from Bozrah?" Where was Bozrah? Turn back to Genesis chapter thirty-six and verse thirty-three: and you will find out where Bozrah was. "And Bela died, and Jacob the son of Zerah of Bozrah reigned in his stead."

It was the capital of one of the kings of Edom. Who were the Edomites? The Edomites were the sons of Esau. Go back to chapter thirty-six of Genesis and verse one: "Now these are the generations of Esau, who is Edom". That word "Bozrah is an interesting word. The word Bozrah means "fortification", "stronghold". The word "Edom" means "red" because when Esau was born he was red, and he also was in opposition to Jacob. He fought with His brother from the birth. And "red" in scripture is a type of sin.

Turn over to Isaiah chapter one and you read these words: "From the sole of the foot even unto the head there is no soundness in it; but wounds and bruises, and putrefying sores: they have not been closed, neither bound up, neither mollified with ointment" (verse six). Then verse eighteen: Come now, and let us reason together; saith the Lord: though your sins be as scarlet, they shall be as white as snow: though they be red like crimson, they shall be as wool". And the word there that is used for red is "Edom" "though they be Edom" "red like crimson". There are two thoughts here "Edom," "red," typical of sin. "Bozrah" "fortification", "stronghold".

What is the result of sin? The result of sin is death. The last great enemy, the fortification, the stronghold, holds men in its deadly grip. I hope you are getting the message. "Who is He that cometh from Edom (His battle with sin), with dyed garments from Bozrah, (His battle with death)" "He that is glorious in His apparel". The garments which Christ wore have endured all the ravages of sin and all the power of death. From the grave He comes, glorious in His apparel, "I that speak in righteousness mighty to save".

Yes, I want to tell you that the garments are glorious because of their endurance.

## 5. THE GARMENT IS GLORIOUS BECAUSE OF ITS INSCRIPTION

We turn back now to Revelation nineteen. In Revelation nineteen it says "He was clothed with a vesture dipped in blood and He has on His vesture a name written".

Now in this portion of scripture there are five names of the Lord.

First of all, verse eleven "He is Faithful".

Secondly, "He is True".

Thirdly, "He is the Word of God".

Fourthly, "He is KING OF KINGS, AND LORD OF LORDS.

Where is the fifth name?

Four is the number of the world, and the Lord Jesus Christ is not of this world.

Look at verse twelve: "He had a name written that no man knew but He Himself". Four names revealed. The world can know those four names. He is Faithful, Hallelujah! We have proved that. He is True. Praise God we have proved that. He is the Word of God. We have proved that. And the world can see He is Faithful. They have seen His people. He is the Word of God. He is KING OF KINGS, AND LORD OF LORDS.

But He has a name that no man knew but He Himself. What is that name? That name is the answer that is given in Isaiah sixty-three. Listen to it: "Who is this?" And then the Lord answers "I that speak in righteousness, mighty to save". Only the believer learns that name. And if you study the book of Revelation you will find that He shares that name with His people.

There is one other thing which I want you to notice, on His vesture and on His thigh He had a name written KING OF KINGS, AND LORD OF LORDS. Very interesting.

In the Old Testament there are types of Christ. The Old Testament believers are never types of Christ in their character. If you ever try to make an Old Testament believer a type of Christ in his character you will be in real trouble. They are only types of Christ in their circumstances, not in their character, for they are all sinners.

There was a man called Jacob and he was going to meet Edom-Esau his brother. Before the dread meeting he wrestled with a man until the dawning of the day. Do you remember it? That man touched his thigh and gave him a new name. He was no longer Jacob but he was Israel, a prince with God.

Now there was a day when the greater Israel went out to meet the Edom of our sins in deadly conflict. When He came back His heel was bruised and He limped upon His thigh like Jacob of old, but He is the KING OF KINGS, AND LORD OF LORDS. And on the vesture dipped in blood there is written in crimson the inscription "KING OF KINGS, AND LORD OF LORDS".

My brethren and sisters in Christ, His apparel is glorious because of its inscription. One day when all the troubles, temptations and trials are fled forever from the people of God I shall stand before Him and I will read the inscription on His vesture dipped in blood "KING OF KINGS, AND LORD OF LORDS". Then shall I join in the Hallelujahs. Please notice those are the only Hallelujahs in the New Testament.

You know when they shouted Hallelujah? They shouted it when Babylon fell. If God's people in this ecumenical age only realised how terrible is the idolatry of the Pope and the tyranny of Vaticanism they would realise the significance of that, Hallelujah.

When the great whore was judged they shouted Hallelujah! Who shouted it? A people in heaven! The voice of much people in heaven, that is who shouted it.

Go down the chapter and you will read "the four and twenty elders!" They represent the whole Church of Christ, twelve apostles of the Lamb for the New Testament, twelve tribes of Israel for the Old Testament. Twenty-four in unison around the Throne shouted Hallelujah! And what else? Four beasts fell down and worshipped God and said "Hallelujah". For the Lord God Omnipotent reigneth. KING OF KINGS! LORD OF LORDS!

What a day that will be when our husky throats will give forth a clear and glorious triumphant shout. When the vaults of heaven will ring and re-echo with the shout of the redeemed. We shall see His face and His name shall be in our foreheads, we shall follow the Lamb whithersoever He doth lead us.

The bride eyes not her garment, But her dear bridegroom's face, I will not gaze at glory, But on the King of grace, Not at the crown He giveth, but on His pierced hand, The Lamb, The Lamb is all the glory in Emmanuel's Land.

And when I study such a subject I feel like old John Bunyan when he described Christian and his companion going in through the gates of heaven - He exclaimed, "I could wish myself among them!"

Thank God some day we will be among them for evermore.

# 7 The disdained garments *of Christ*

**WE HAVE BEEN STUDYING** and meditating on the wardrobe of Christ, the garments which the Saviour wore in the days of His humiliation, and the garments which He now wears in the day of His exaltation.

We commenced our studies in the sixty-third chapter of Isaiah, taking for our theme "The Lord glorious in His apparel".

We looked at The Distinctive Garments of Christ. The first garment that pressed upon His baby flesh was the swaddling clothes, a type of shroud, and of course Jesus Christ was born to die. "To this end was I born, for this purpose came I into the world!"

We saw also that His garments in the service of His ministry were marked with the hem. The hem is the finished work, and when those that were diseased touched the hem of His garment they were immediately made whole.

We moved then to consider The Distinguished Garments of Christ, and we have had quite a number of messages on these distinguished garments of Christ.

We come to a new part of our study. We are going to look at *The Disdained Garments of Christ*. These garments are two in number.

Turn with me please to Luke's gospel chapter twenty-three and verse eleven, "And Herod with his men of war set Him at nought, and mocked Him, and arrayed Him in a gorgeous robe". Mark it: "Arrayed Him in a gorgeous robe and sent Him again to Pilate!"

Then turn to John's gospel chapter nineteen, and we read there in verse two: "And the soldiers platted a crown of thorns, and put it on His head, and they put on Him a purple robe".

So He was robed by Herod in a gorgeous robe, He was robed by Pilate's soldiers in a robe of purple.

Check in Matthew's gospel chapter twenty-seven and verse twenty-eight: "And they stripped Him, and put on Him a scarlet robe". So He was dressed in purple and scarlet by Pilate's men, and He was dressed in a gorgeous robe by the men of Herod.

You know if you study the Word of God you will find that the Bible divides the human family into two and into two only.

Romans chapter two emphasises this and gives us the division. Now if you turn with me to that chapter and mark these verses, they will teach you this division of the human race. Romans chapter two and verse nine: "Tribulation and anguish, upon every soul of man that doeth evil!" This takes in the whole human race "on every soul of man that doeth evil, of the Jew first, and also to the Gentile!" Look at verse ten: "But glory, honour, and peace, to every man that worketh good, to the Jew first, and also to the Gentile!" And then if you turn to Romans chapter three and verse nine you have the division again: "What then? are we better than they? No, in no wise: for we have before proved both Jews and Gentiles, that they are all under sin".

So there is only a twofold division in the scriptures of the human race of unbelievers, Jews and Gentiles. Of course, when we come to the Church we have another division. We have the Jews, the Gentiles and the Church of God. But I am talking now about the division of unbelievers.

Now when you study the death of the Lord Jesus Christ you will find that He was tried by the Jewish people in a threefold trial.

**THE TRIALS OF OUR SAVIOUR**

His first trial by the Jewish people is found in John's gospel chapter eighteen. There you have His first trial by the Jewish people. Verse twelve: "Then the band of the captain and officers of the Jews took Jesus, and bound Him. And led Him away to Annas first; for he was the father-in-law to Caiaphas, who was the high priest that year!" Then He was taken before Caiaphas, and you have His trial before Caiaphas recorded in Matthew chapter twenty-six verses fifty-nine to sixty -three.

Then last of all He is taken to the king, the king of the Jews, the son of Herod the Great. He is brought in Luke's gospel chapter twenty-three before Herod.

So He had a threefold trial before the Jewish people. Before Annas, Caiaphas and Herod.

Then He was tried before the Gentile people by Pilate. Now you will notice if you study carefully, that there is a repetition in what the Jews did to Christ and what the Gentiles did to Christ.

First of all look with me at John's gospel chapter eighteen and verse twenty-two, and you will find that when He was before the Jews. "And when He had thus spoken, one of the officers which stood by struck Jesus with the palm of his hand". He was struck with the palm of the hand by these Jews.

Then if you turn over to verse three of John's gospel chapter nineteen, you will find that the Gentiles also struck Him with the palm of the hand. Look at verse three "And they smote Him with their hands".

So the Jews smote Jesus with their hands and then the Gentiles followed suit.

The Lord Jesus Christ was spat upon by both Jews and Gentiles. Twice He was spat upon. Turn over to Matthew chapter twenty-six and in verse sixty-seven, we read that when He was before Caiaphas; "Then did they spit in His face". So He was spat upon by the Jewish people.

Turn over to Matthew chapter twenty-seven and verse thirty, and you read there "And they spit upon Him". Again the Gentiles follow suit.

So both Jews and Gentiles struck Him with the palms of their hands. Both Jews and Gentiles spat upon Him.

Go back to Luke's gospel chapter twenty-three and verse eleven and you find there that Pilate's men mocked the Lord Jesus Christ. "Herod with his men of war set Him at nought and mocked Him". Then turn over to Matthew chapter twenty-seven and verse nine and you will read that Pilate's soldiers mocked Him.

So He was spat upon twice. He was struck twice and He was mocked twice.

But the parallel runs on. He was robed twice. He was robed by both Jews and Gentiles. I want you to see the significance of this, for it is of vital importance if we are going to grasp the spiritual teaching of these robings which took place.

In Luke's gospel chapter twenty-three and verse eleven, "they arrayed Him in a gorgeous robe". Then we turn over to Matthew and compare it with John's gospel He was arrayed by Pilate in a robe of purple and of scarlet.

So we have the robing of Christ by the Jewish people with Herod as their head and king, and we have the robing of Christ by the Gentile people with Pilate as their head.

## A MOST INTERESTING WORD

This word "gorgeous" is a most interesting word. This is the only place in the New Testament that it is translated in our Authorised Version by the word "gorgeous". As a matter of fact it occurs nine times only in the New Testament. It is translated twice by the word "bright". I want you to look at these two passages of scripture because they bring out the real meaning of this word "gorgeous".

Acts chapter ten and verse thirty: "And Cornelius said, Four days ago I was fasting until this hour: and at the ninth hour I prayed in my house, and behold, a man stood before me in *bright* clothing". Now the word which is translated "bright" in that passage is the same word which is translated "gorgeous" about the robe that was put on Christ by Herod's men.

If you turn over to Revelation twenty-two and verse sixteen, you will find that that word occurs again. It says of Jesus Christ, "I am the root and the off-spring of David, and the *bright* and morning star". That is the same word. So twice it is translated "bright".

Once it is translated by the word "clear". Turn to Revelation twenty-two and verse one, "And he shewed me a pure river of water of life, *clear* as crystal". That is the same word which is translated "gorgeous" about the robe which Herod put on Christ. It is translated once by "clear".

It is translated once by the word "gay". Turn over to James chapter two, and in verse three we read "And ye have respect to him that weareth the *gay* clothing". That word "gay" is the same word which is translated "gorgeous".

It is translated twice by "goodly". In James chapter two and verse two, "For if there come unto your assembly a man with a gold ring, in *goodly* apparel". The same word "goodly apparel". It is translated again by the word "goodly" in Revelation eighteen and verse fourteen: "And the fruits that thy soul lusted after are departed from thee, and all things which were dainty and *goodly*". This is the same word.

Then last of all it is translated over in Revelation by the word "white". Turn to Revelation chapter fifteen and verse six, "And the seven angels came out of the temple, having the seven plagues, clothed in pure and *white* linen". That word "white" is the word which is translated "gorgeous" in this passage concerning the robe.

The last reference is Revelation nineteen and verse eight, which we have looked at before. It describes the linen which the people of God wear in heaven, and it says "she should be arrayed in fine linen, clean and *white*". That is the same word.

So the robe which Herod put upon the Lord Jesus Christ was a white robe, bright and shining. Now what does that robe represent? The only people in the East who wore the bright, dazzling white robes were the kings of the East. It was a kingly robe. It probably was one of Herod's own robes. How do I know that? Because if you turn over to Psalm sixty-eight, you will find the proof. It is a good thing for us to search the scriptures. Psalm sixty-eight and verse fourteen says: "When the Almighty scattered kings in it, it was white as snow in Salmon". So when the kings were slaughtered and lay dead on the mountain side, it was like snow. Why? Because all of them wore the white garments.

White is the kingly garment. That is why the Lord Jesus Christ when He was preaching about the glories of Solomon said, "Consider the lilies of the field, they toil not, nether do they spin, nor gather into barns. Yet Solomon in all his glory was not arrayed like one of these," the white lilies, because the king wore the white robe.

So the Jewish people, in the person of Herod and his men of war, put upon Christ the kingly robe, the robe that the king of the Jews would have worn.

Now we come to the Gentiles. The Gentiles did not clothe their kings in white. They clothed their kings in purple and scarlet. You see there is a great difference. We are coming from one nation to another. We are coming from one type of raiment to another type of raiment.

Purple and scarlet are the colours of the kings of the Gentiles. If you go and have a look at the woman who controls the kings of the earth, (Revelation chapter seventeen verse four), how is she attired? She is attired in purple and scarlet. Now if you go right down to the next chapter you will find the purple and the scarlet (Revelation chapter eighteen verse twelve). Get this and mark it well. The royal robe of the Gentiles was purple and scarlet.

The royal robe of the Lord Jesus Christ as King of the Jews was white. So He was dressed in both kingly robes.

The clothing of Christ in mockery in these robes denotes *first of all the total depravity of the whole human race*.

Both Jews and Gentiles, both the sacred and the secular joined together to robe Him in cruel mockery of His claims as KING OF KINGS, AND LORD OF LORDS. Oh the ignominy to which sin put my Saviour! Oh the shame that my Lord was subjected to when cruel men mocked His claims and arrayed Him in a kingly robe and derided His Kingship. The whole race is branded in these robes for their depravity and sin.

You know, of course, they did not know what they were doing. The Lord Jesus Christ, when those robes were put upon Him, was simply displaying His Person and His Character. Turn over to the Song of Solomon chapter five and verse nine, "What is thy beloved more than another beloved, O thou fairest among women? What is thy beloved more than another beloved, that thou dost so charge us? My beloved is white". He wore a white robe first. You know the scriptures were not written by men, because if man had written those scriptures the order would not have mattered. He could have written, "my beloved is ruddy and white, the chiefest among then thousand".

*The white robe was worn first*

Why? It depicts His spotless character as the King of the Jews, for from the Jewish race was to come God's Lamb, God's spotless, crimeless, sinless, flawless Lamb to take away our sin.

"My beloved is white, and ruddy". The purple and scarlet bring out the full crimson and red of His precious blood in the passion of the cross.

Before He could don the robe of blood shedding He must clothe Himself by his character and life. He was the Lamb of God. And if you go back to Exodus you will find that the Lamb had to be taken out from the flock, and it had to be kept in a separate place for a considerable time to prove it had not a spot, that it had no blemish. (Exodus chapter twelve verses five and six).

Evil men put upon Him a white shining robe, but little did they know when they put it on Him that they were declaring His innocence.

I want to tell you something more. Old Pilate saw something more than the unbelieving Jew saw, for if you turn over to the eighteenth and nineteenth chapters of John, three times Pilate says "I find no fault in Him". Look at John eighteen and verse thirty-eight, "I find in Him no fault at all". Look at verse four of John nineteen: "I find no fault in Him". Look at verse six: "I find no fault in Him".

Three is the number of completion in the Word of God. Nothing is complete in scripture which is not characterised by the number three. That is why the Lord's death is a complete death, for He was buried three days and three nights. It is a perfect sacrifice.

The number three is important. Three times the fact is witnessed that He is innocent.

When you turn over to Luke's gospel chapter twenty-three and verse fourteen you will find something more. When Christ came back from Herod what did Pilate say? "I have examined Him before you, and I have found no fault in this man no nor yet Herod". What did Pilate learn from the white robe which Herod put upon Christ? That the Lord Jesus Christ was absolutely innocent.

Wicked men did not know what they were doing, but God knew. They put upon Him the gorgeous robe, the white robe. "My beloved is white".

*Then they put on Him the purple robe*

It speaks of His death. The purple robe is, however, linked with something else, it is linked with the crown of thorns. (I have no time to deal with the significance of that link. That is a subject for a message all on its own.) But the crown of thorns and the purple robe are linked together because "my beloved is white" that is His innocence, "and He is ruddy", He is the sacrificed King.

You know what Pilate did? He wrote an inscription and put it over the cross "This is the King of the Jews!" Little did Pilate think when he wrote that that he was writing God's truth. "For He has made Him a little lower than the angels, for the sufferings of death, and crowned Him with glory and honour". (Hebrews chapter two verse nine).

The purple robe and the crown of thorns signified another coronation, when every thorn of the curse (Genesis three verse eighteen) would be withdrawn from men, when they repented and were redeemed, and when they would stand as courtiers before the KING OF KINGS, AND LORD OF LORDS.

These robes display the Person and Character of Christ. They do something else. They designate the transfer of final power when the kingdoms of this world become the kingdoms of the Lord Jesus Christ.

Herod the king puts on Christ the kingly robe because the Bible says that the lawgiver shall not depart from Judah until Shiloh comes, and unto Him shall the gathering of the people be. That signified the end of the reign of the Jewish people with a king. That was the end. Yes! Because Shiloh had come. Herod, that day, when he took the kingly robe and put it on Christ, signified the final transfer of kingly power from Israel to the Saviour.

There is only One who can occupy the Throne of His father David, and that One is the Lord Jesus Christ.

## THE TRANSFER OF POWER

If you turn over to Genesis chapter forty-one you will find that the transfer of power is made by the raiment which is given to the person that is so exalted. Genesis chapter forty-one and verse thirty-nine. It is about Joseph, and what does it say? "And Pharaoh said unto his servants, 'Can we find such a one as this, a man in whom the Spirit of God is?'" (Genesis forty-one and verse thirty-eight). "And Pharaoh said unto Joseph, 'Forasmuch as God hath shewed thee all this, there is none so discreet and wise as thou art: Thou shalt be over my house, and according unto thy word shall all my people be ruled: only in the throne will I be greater than thou'. And Pharaoh said unto Joseph, 'See, I have set thee over all the land of Egypt.' And Pharaoh took off his ring form his hand, and put it upon Joseph's hand, and arrayed him in vestures of fine linen." The word there is "white". He has got the white robe. The transfer of power. That is it.

Turn over to Daniel and you will find that the transfer of power was made by the giving of the robe. You will remember when Daniel read the writings that were upon the wall, what did they do? Of course Daniel was now among the Gentile races. "Then commanded Belshazzar, and they clothed Daniel with scarlet, and put a chain of gold about his neck, and made a proclamation". And as

Joseph is a type of Christ, and got the rulership with the white robe, Daniel also is a type of Christ and he got the rulership with the scarlet robe.

Of course that brings us to the story of the four great world kingdoms which I want to talk about. The kingdom of Babylon, the kingdom of the Medes and Persians, the kingdom of the Grecians and the kingdom of the Romans.

Thank God there is a day coming when a stone not cut out with hands will smite the image upon its feet, and the kingdoms of this world shall become the kingdoms of the Lord and of His Christ, and He shall reign. The transfer of power. "All power is given unto me in heaven and in earth".

They crowned Him in their folly and in their sin, but little did they know that in those disdainful garments my Lord was simply showing forth His princely power and kingly glory.

**HE WALKED AS KING**

One last thought. The last time Jesus walked through the streets of Jerusalem, He walked as a king. His procession was from the palace of Herod to the judgment hall of Pilate. That is the last time He walked through old Jerusalem, from one end to the other, for Pilate's judgment hall and Herod's palace were far apart. His journey to Calvary was outside the city walls, down the narrow streets.

The last time He traversed the whole city He traversed it in the garments of the king. Is it not significant that He was revealed to Israel as the King before He went to the sufferings of the cross.

There is another day coming when my Lord shall be revealed once again to the stumbling, unbelieving Jews as the King. Then shall a nation be born in a day, and then shall God graft in again those branches which were cut out because of unbelief. What a day, when in the gorgeous robes from the Father's wardrobe, and with the purple robes, the vesture dipped in blood, He shall appear to His people. Notice the two colours in the vesture in heaven. It is a vesture of fine linen - that is white, but it is dipped in blood - that is purple. The two garments are brought together in the final coronation garment of Christ, and He rides upon the white horse when He comes to reign over this old world of ours.

"Oh the crowning day is coming, is coming by and by."

This week, one of my twin sons young Kyle, as he was going to school in the morning, said to his mother, "Mammy, I can't wait until I get to heaven!" Mammy said "Why?" He replied "I just long to see the cape which Jesus wears!" The message was getting home to his young heart!

May we long to see the Saviour. May we long to see Him face to face, and tell the story saved by grace. Amen and Amen.

# 8 The discarded garments *of Christ*

**I WANT TO CONTINUE** the series of messages that I have been giving on "The Wardrobe of Christ or "The Wonderful Garments of our Wonderful Lord". We had, first of all, a look at *The Distinctive Garments* of Christ.

We noted that the first garment that ever pressed upon His baby body, when He was born of the virgin, was the linen shroud or swaddling clothes. Typical not of birth, but of death. When born He was wrapped in a shroud, in fulfilment of His own personal testimony "To this end was I born, and for this purpose came I into the world". His birth was in order to His bleeding, and His cradle was in order to the cross.

We also noted that the garment that was seen of men, as He walked around this sin cursed scene of time, was the garment with the hem "And as many as touched the hem of His garment, were immediately made whole". The women folk know that the hem is the finished work. When the garment is completed then it is hemmed and finished. So that hem was typical of the finished work of the Lord Jesus Christ. For it is only by His death we live, and through His blood we have pardon from sin.

We then moved on to discuss *The Distinguished Garments* of Christ. We had a look at His everyday clothing. The five garments of the Galilean peasant. The headdress, the sandals, the outer coat, the girdle and the inner vestment. All very suggestive and full of wonderful teaching about our wonderful and blessed Lord.

We consider also His garments in the glory. We saw in Revelation chapter one: "Clothed from head to foot, girt about the paps with a golden girdle". The girdle, of course, was always worn about the loins. And, of course, in the Eastern country, when the man went forth to his work, he girded up his long flowing robes about the leather girdle that was about his loins. It was a sign of strength and work to do. You will remember that Elijah girded himself and ran before the chariot of Ahab. The Lord Jesus no longer wears the girdle around His loins because His work is done, "It is finished, was His cry. Now in heaven exalted high, Hallelujah what a Saviour". He wears the girdle around His breast. It has become the breastplate of our glorious high priest, Who bore the names of His people upon His breast.
"My name from the palms of His hands. Eternity will not erase, Impressed on His heart it remains, in marks of indelible grace. Yes, I to the end shall endure as sure as the earnest is given, More happy but not more secure, 'Till glorified with Him in heaven".

We also looked at the distinguished garment in which our Lord will come again. Because we, in this church, believe in the second personal return of the Lord Jesus Christ to this earth, in power and great glory: "This same Jesus, whom ye have seen go into heaven, shall so come in like manner as ye have seen Him go into heaven. Every eye shall see Him, and those also that pierced Him". And that pre-supposes the resurrection of the unjust.

We have looked at the garment in which He comes, it is a vestment dipped in blood.

Then we looked at *the Disdained Garments* of Christ. The garments that He wore because of His mocking. The garment that was put upon Him by Herod the Judean monarch, the Jewish monarch. And then the garment that was put upon Him by Pilate representing Caesar, the purple robe.

We had a look at these two disdained garments of our Lord.

We are coming now to speak on another very interesting and instructive subject: The Discarded Garments of Christ.

On four occasions only the Lord Jesus Christ discarded His garments. The first one was a voluntary discarding of His garments. He did it voluntarily. The last one was of the same character. But the two in between were inflicted upon Him by the hands of men.

## DISCARDED FOR SERVICE

Now let us look at the first one in John thirteen. The thirteenth chapter of John's gospel, and it says there: "He riseth from supper, (verse four) and laid aside His garments; and took a towel, and girded Himself". You can write over that "The Lord's garments discarded for *service*. Now turn with me to Matthew chapter twenty-seven and verse twenty-eight; and there we read these words: "And they stripped Him". There we find they were discarded for *suffering*. Before His mocking and His beating, and His battering, and His scourging in Pilate's Hall, His garments were discarded; discarded for suffering. Turn to John's gospel chapter nineteen and verse twenty-three, we read these words: "Then the soldiers, when they had crucified Jesus, took His garments!" Discarded for *sacrifice*. And then turn over a little farther in John's gospel, and you will come to the last discarding of His garments: John twenty and verse six "Then cometh Simon Peter following Him, and went into the sepulchre, and seeth the linen clothes lie, and the napkin that was about His head, not lying with the linen clothes, but wrapped together in a place by itself. Then went in also that other disciple, which came first to the sepulchre, and he saw, and believed". So the Lord discarded the graveclothes. Discarded for *sovereignty*. For He is the Sovereign Lord. He has conquered death, and hell, and the grave. And He lives in the power of an endless life.

So we have these four discardings of our Lord's garments. Discarded willingly and voluntarily to do the work of a slave. Discarded by the hands of men on two occasions: for the scourging, for the crucifying. And then the garments that He wore in death were discarded on the day of resurrection.

Now I want to come to the first one please, in John's gospel chapter thirteen. This is a most interesting study. It was the duty of the slave in the eastern country to wash the feet of all that came to supper. Because those that had traversed the roads, although they had washed themselves in preparation for the meal, when they arrived to supper their feet were dirty. So the first duty of the slave was to wash the feet of the guest. Turn over to Luke's gospel chapter seventeen, and there you will find a word which confirms that. Luke's gospel seventeen, verses seven and eight: "But which of you, having a servant plowing or feeding cattle, will say unto him by and by, when he is come from the field Go and sit down to meat? And will not rather say unto him, Make ready wherewith I may sup, and gird myself, and serve me, till I have eaten and drunken; and afterwards thou shalt eat and drink?"

So the first duty of the servant was to gird himself, and wash the feet of those who had come to supper. Now the disciples had come to the supper. And I can see them all looking at one another. Peter says: "Well if James thinks I am going to be the servant, and take the basin and the towel and wash their feet, he has another think coming to him. I am not going to do any such thing". And John says: "Well I am the youngest of the disciples, if they think they are just going to make a little boy out of me, then can think again. I am not going to wash the feet." And then something happened. They had sat down at the table for the first meal, not the Passover Supper. For the first meal before they ate of the Passover Supper. And the Lord Jesus Christ Himself rose. Notice the beauty of the language: "And riseth from supper". Why? Because there is something missing. The disciples, the guest, had not had the necessary refreshment in feet washing. "And He laid aside His garments, and took a towel, and girded Himself. After that He poureth water into a basin, and began to wash the disciples' feet, and to wipe them with the towel wherewith He was girded". And then look down the chapter to verse twelve: "So after He had washed their feet, and had taken His garments, and was set down again, He said unto them, 'Know ye what I have done to you? Ye call me Master and Lord: and ye say well; for so I am. If I then, your Lord and Master, have washed your feet; ye also ought to wash one another's feet'".

There is a beautiful type here. How did the Lord Jesus cleanse us? How did He do it? He rose one day, and He left aside the garments of His glory, the garments in which the angels saw Him, the garments which were the garments of the Prince of heaven, the only begotten of the Father. And He took upon Him the form of a servant: Philippians chapter two: "Who being in the form of God, thought it not robbery to be equal with God: but took upon Him the form of a servant." He girded Himself with a towel and He humbled Himself. How did the Lord wash the disciples' feet? He knelt down before them! A prostate Lord before sinners that sinned. That is a perfect type of grace. Instead of sinners prostrate before their Maker, here we have the Lord prostrate, on His knees, before sinners. "And He poured water into the basin". And out of His side flowed water and blood for the cleansing of the world. And I want you to notice something. The water was not lost that was in the basin. Not any of my Saviour's water and blood was lost in the shedding at Calvary. It is all preserved. What for? For the washing of His church. And then there is something more. After He had cleansed them all, what did He do? He put on His garments again. My Lord once appeared as a servant, but He is no longer the servant today. He is robed again in the splendid attire of heaven's praised and of heaven's glory. And the highest placing that heaven affords is His by sovereign right, the KING OF KINGS, AND LORD OF LORDS, He reigns in perfect light. There is a perfect type here. But I want you to look a little closer at this, for it deserves even closer attention.

*First of all that the Lord serves His people*

He did not take the place of the Master, and command one of the disciples to do to the work of the slave. But He Himself took the position of servant, the Lord served His people. And while His humiliation is now past, and He is in the glory of His exaltation, Praise God, the Lord still serves His people. He is still at the service of the church. He is still as willing to deal with the problems and with the perplexities that the church may have. Remember, the Lord is at our service.

*Secondly, Nothing is too small for the attention of the Saviour*

It seemed a small thing, that the disciples' feet were not washed. Something that could on this occasion, be well overlooked. After all, was He not going to leave this room and kneel amid the olive groves of Gethsemane, and sweat great drops of blood falling down to the ground. Was He not going to be taken, that very night, from prison into judgment, and the following morning to hang upon the cross, in agony and blood shedding? Surely, the all importance of Gethsemane and the all importance of Calvary, would put the petty thing of washing the disciples' feet out of His mind. But not so with the Lord. The Lord Jesus is concerned with the whole of this world, with the archangels and the hosts of archangels who do His commission, and carry out His plans and I want to tell you He is interested in His disciples' feet.

The feet of course speak of *the path*, don't they? And *the Lord is interested in the path that you walk.* Perhaps that path, this week, has brought you along the valley of suffering. But the Lord is interested in your path. Perhaps you have walked the road of disappointment. Is there someone here, and this week you have almost been crushed under the load of disappointment? The Lord is interested in your feet, in your path. Maybe there is someone here, and you have stood this week over the grave of a loved one, the hot tear has fallen down your cheeks, and you have left that graveside as if you have buried all your hopes under the gravedigger's spade. But the Lord is interested in your path. He knows, He cares, He understands, He is the only One Who is prepared to give you refreshment this morning, and to kneel at your feet to cleanse away the dust that has accumulated on your path, to take the thorns that have penetrated your feet as you walked a bitter highway. The Lord is interested today in you!

*Thirdly, The Lord is here concerned about the purity of His people*

He desires nothing more than this, than that they should be clean. And you will notice that impetuous Peter said "Lord, you will not wash my feet". And the Lord said: "If I do not wash your feet, you have no part in me". And then he says "Not my feet, but my hands and my head also". And what does the Lord say, I want you to look at it "He that is washed needeth not save to wash his feet, but is clean every whit; and ye are clean, but not all". For He knew who should betray Him; therefore said He "Ye are not all clean". Do you not notice that the Lord had one concern, and that was for the purity of His disciples? And He knelt even before Judas, as He washed Judas's feet. The very feet that were going to carry Judas to the Temple to take the blood money that was to be the bribe of betrayal. Why? Because the Lord is full of grace, and the Lord is full of love. He could have passed Judas by. You know that word in the Passover Supper "He that dippeth his hand with me in the dish, the same will betray me". And in the Jewish Passover, it was the man who was most beloved that dipped his finger in the dish with the host of the supper. And the Lord gave Judas the place that was most distinguished. The Lord at the feet of Judas, the Lord dipping His hand with Judas in the dish. Why? Because God is a God of grace. A God of love. He is not ready to judge men. He is not willing to judge men in haste. He reaches out after them. He longs that they might turn to Him and feel the power of His pardon.

If the Lord Jesus was willing to kneel before Judas, knowing that Judas would betray Him, if He was willing to dip His hand with Judas in the dish, knowing that Judas's hand would soon have the blood money for His betrayal, let me tell you how much more willing He is to succour His own people, those that are redeemed by His blood, and saved by His grace. I want you to notice something more, it is only the Lord Who can do this cleansing. He has discarded His garments, He has girded Himself with a towel, He kneels before His church today. He comes to wipe away and wash away the imperfections of our walk, to wash away the dirt that we have accumulated as we have traversed life's rugged pathway, to make us clean and refresh us, so that when we go out we can go out washed and cleansed by His grace, and refreshed by His presence.

## DISCARDED FOR SUFFERING

The second point I want to make: Matthew twenty-seven and verse twenty-eight: "And they stripped Him. Here we have *His garments discarded for suffering*. This was the prelude to our Lord's shame: "And when they had platted a crown of thorns, they put it upon His head, and a reed in His right hand; and they bowed the knee before Him, and mocked Him saying, Hail, King of the Jews! And they spit upon Him, and took the reed, and smote Him on the head. And after that they had mocked Him". I want you to notice the sad catalogue of sufferings which the Lord endured. Turn over with me to John's gospel, and you will read these words, "Then Pilate therefore took Jesus, and scourged Him" (John chapter nineteen). That is what happened when a man was crucified, he was first scourged. They took away His garments, they tied His wrists together with a leather thong, they brought him to a pole which was known as the scourging pole. It was so elevated that as the victim was pushed over it, his feet just trailed upon the ground. So the Lord Jesus Christ after being crowned with thorns, and spit upon, and mocked, is put over the scourging pole, His wrists are tied, His back is bent, He is trailing His feet upon the ground. And then the Roman soldier, cruel blasphemous man, lifts the leather thong, something like the "cat of nine tails" and on every thong there was a piece of bone, carefully interwoven into the leather, so that when the thong came down upon the victim, instead of laying a welt it opened a wound in the back. That is why the prophet said: "They plowed furrows upon my back. And I hear the swish of the lash, and I see the precious, naked body of my Lord scourged with the scourge as the rivers of blood flow down, and He is clothed with another garment, the garment of His own precious blood.

Let me ask you something:

"Was it for me, for me alone, The Saviour left His glorious Throne, The dazzling splendour of the sky, Was it for me, He came to die?" Why was my Saviour lashed, and scourged, and mocked in Pilate's Judgment Hall? Why was my Saviour to submit Himself to such mockery and shame? It was for you and it was for me. Discarded for suffering!"

Could I bring you from Gabbatha with its scourging, to Golgotha with its crucifying? Here again at the cross they stripped Him. Of course between times they had put on His garments, and His garments were now soaked with His own blood, especially the inner garment, the vesture, which was dipped in blood, it was soaked with the blood shedding as a result of His scourging. That is why it says in Revelation "His vesture was dipped in blood". They took those garments off Him again, and they opened up every river of congealed blood upon His back. And I see them taking those garments and stripping them from off the blessed Saviour. "Who is this that cometh from Edom, with dyed garments from Bozrah?" "Why art Thou red in Thine apparel, like Him that treadeth in the winefat?" The prophet's words were completely and absolutely fulfilled. And then what happened? Having taken His garments from off him, "I hear the sound of the hammer swung low. They are nailing my Lord to the tree."

Was it for me He wept and prayed, My load of sin upon Him laid. That night within Gethsemane, Was it for me that agony? Was it for me He bowed His head, upon that cross and freely shed, His precious blood, that crimson tide, Was it for me my Saviour died?

It was for me, it was for me, and it was for you.

Have you ever knelt at that cross and gazed upon the suffering Son of God, and thanked Him that having loved His own, He loved them unto the end?

As we continue our study we will have a look at the discarded garments of that tomb, a wonderful study. I would like you to think about one thing: Why was the napkin wrapped and placed by itself? Think on these things and God will bless them to your soul.

Maybe you have not trusted the Saviour as yet. Let me tell you His hands are outstretched to you today, and all you have got to do is come to Him, and "Him that cometh unto me" said the Saviour, "I will in no wise cast out".

# 9 The disgarded garments *of Christ*

**TURN TO JOHN'S GOSPEL** chapter nineteen and the verses thirty-eight to forty-two.

We come to the most intriguing, the most instructive and the most exciting of all subjects that we have discussed in regard to our Lord's Garments.

Could I just briefly remind you that we have dealt in this series of messages with The Lord's *Distinctive* Garments, that is the garments that He wore of special distinction. Swaddling clothes, the first clothes that pressed upon His baby flesh, a type and a symbol of death, for the Lord was born to die.

Then of course His every day garment. His outer garment had a hem, and as many as touched the hem of His garment were made perfectly whole. The hem is the finished work and it is through the finished work of Christ that sinners are made perfectly whole.

Then we looked at The *Distinguished* Garments of Christ. The five garments which He wore and especially the vesture upon which they did cast lots.

We looked at The *Disdained* Garments of Christ. The purple robe and the scarlet robe. Now we have come to look at The *Discarded* Garments of Christ.

Four times in the scriptures He discarded his garments. He laid them aside when He girded Himself with a towel to do the work of a slave. Discarded for service.

They were laid aside in Pilate's judgment hall that He might be scourged. Discarded for suffering.

They were laid aside at Calvary. Discarded for sacrifice.

Now we come to the discarding of our Lord's funeral garments. His grave clothes. They were discarded for Sovereignty. For He laid them aside to declare to heaven, earth and sky that He is the One that liveth and was dead, and behold, He is alive for evermore.

## DISCARDED FOR SOVEREIGNTY

I want you to look with me then at the discarding of the Lord's garments for Sovereignty.

There are four numbers in the scriptures that should always be kept in mind when we come to consider the doctrine of the resurrection of the Lord Jesus.

The first number is the number of one or the first.

The second number is the number two or the second.

The third is the number three or the third and the fourth is the number eight or the eighth.

One, two, three and eight are all numbers surrounding the resurrection of the Lord Jesus Christ, and indeed the doctrine of the resurrection in the scriptures.

If you turn over to Mark sixteen and verse nine, you have there a verse that completely and absolutely breaks up any thought that there is any significance in Seventh Day Adventism. It says in verse nine of Mark sixteen "Now when

Jesus was risen early, the first day of the week". So the Lord Jesus Christ rose from the dead on the first day of the week.

As I have pointed out in these studies it is important to remember a basic law in Biblical interpretation. That is the law of the first mention. The first time a day, or a number, or a name, or a city, or a river, or a tree is mentioned in the Bible gives the key to every other mention of the particular object.

Turn over to Genesis chapter one and you will find that something happened on the first day of creation. Before the first day of creation the earth was without form and void, and darkness was upon the face of the deep. That is a description, is it not, of death? Darkness upon the face of the deep. But there is something else. The Spirit of God was moving. And then on the first day God said "Let there be light". A light shone. A perfect type of resurrection. The darkness gave place to light. Jesus Christ on the first day of the week, the Light of the world came out of the darkness of the depths of death and thank God shed forth His light across the earth. How did He come forth? He came forth by the Spirit of God. "Who by the Spirit of God came forth from the dead". And so in the law of the first mention we have anticipated and have in beautiful type the doctrine of the resurrection.

**THE FIRST**

If you study the New Testament you will find that the word "first" occurs in regard to the resurrection of Christ. Acts twenty-six and verse twenty-three: He is the first to rise from the dead.

When I was a boy and when I first read that scripture I said "That is not true. There were other people who rose from the dead". Yes, it is true for every other person that rose from the dead went back into the grave. It was very nice for Lazarus to have a resurrection but he had to die over again. He had two deaths. But the Lord Jesus Christ was the first to leave the tomb and never return. This is what it means. The first to arise from the dead.

In Revelation chapter one and verse five He is called "the first begotten of the dead".

In Colossians chapter one and verse eighteen He is called "the firstborn from the dead".

In I Corinthians fifteen and verse twenty He is called "the firstfruits of them that slept".

The number one or the first is very important in any study of the resurrection of Christ.

**THE SECOND**

The next number is the number two, and that is very important in any study of the resurrection of Christ.

Turn over to Deuteronomy chapter seventeen and verse six. You will find that under the Mosaic law the only witness that was sufficient was a witness of two or three persons. Of course the greatest fact in history is the fact of the Lord's resurrection. And we have a series of two. Deuteronomy chapter seventeen and verse six: "At the mouth of two witnesses or three witnesses, shall he that is worthy of death be put to death; but at the mouth of one witness he shall not be put to death". And the Mosaic law carried it a bit farther in their tradition, and they would not allow a woman to be a witness. So if two women gunned up on you under the Mosaic law their witness was not accepted. And of course this is carried on even when the apostle Paul is speaking about the resurrection. Turn over to I Corinthians, the great chapter of the resurrection, I Corinthians chapter fifteen and verse five. You will find that He does not mention any of the women that saw the resurrection. He did not mention them! "And that He was seen of Cephas, then of the twelve: After that, He was seen of above five hundred brethren at once". No woman mentioned! "Five hundred brethren at once, of whom the greater part remained, but after that He was seen of James; then of all the apostles. And last of all He was seen of me also". That was how Paul the Jew, in order to establish the resurrection of Christ retains the Mosaic tradition that no woman could be a witness. So he only brings the witness of the men who saw Jesus after He was risen.

Now if you look carefully at the resurrection narratives you will find that there is a series of eight "twos".

Two men prepared His body for the burial. Joseph and Nicodemus.

Two men, Peter and John, entered into the tomb.

Two Marys were reported by John in association with His resurrection.

Mary of Bethany in John twelve and verses one to nine. She anointed Christ for His burial. Mary Magdalene was there at the tomb in John twenty and verse one.

Two Marys are reported by Matthew as witnessing our Lord's burial. Matthew twenty-seven and verse sixty-one says that Mary Magdalene and the other Mary watched the burial service of Christ.

Two Marys are reported by Matthew as coming to see the sepulchre. Matthew twenty-eight and verse one.

Two angels are reported sitting after the resurrection. One sat on a stone outside the tomb. (Matthew twenty-eight and verse two) and one sat on the right side of where Christ lay. (Mark sixteen and verse five).

Two standing angels. Their posture is very important.

Two standing angels are reported in Luke chapter twenty-four and verse four.

Two sitting angels are reported in John chapter twenty and verse twelve. "One at the head, and the other at the feet, where the body of Jesus had lain."

There are eight "twos". We will come to the importance of eight in a moment or two.

Could I say something to you. If you study the New Testament you will find that there were fourteen appearances of the Lord Jesus Christ after His resurrection. Fourteen! Fourteen is made up of seven multiplied by two. Seven is the number of perfection. Two is the number of witness. So fourteen is a perfection of perfection. A perfect witness. (I have no time to go over these fourteens).

The Lord Jesus is going to be seen again. Thank God every believer is going to see Him. That will be His fifteenth appearance. Fifteen is made up of three multiplied by five. Five is the number of grace. Three is the number of completion. Praise God in the fifteenth appearance grace will have come to completion. And when grace comes to completion that will be glory for me! That is what glory is. Glory is grace completed.

## THE THIRD

Then of course we come to the third day. And of course the third day is worthy of mention.

Could I say in the law of the first mention the second day is the day when the heaven was made. And the first thing that we read that God put in the heavens after creation was the rainbow. A witness that He would never again destroy the world by a flood. So on the second day heaven was made and the first thing that God put in the heaven after creation was the rainbow. A token, a witness of His covenant.

Turn to the third day in Genesis and you have a beautiful type of the resurrection. Genesis chapter one and verse nine: "And God said, Let the waters under the heaven be gathered together unto one place, and let the dry land appear: and it was so". Can you imagine this world a sea without a shore, an ocean without a boundary? And then suddenly the seas recede and the mountains appear and then the dry land appears. That is a perfect type of resurrection, is it not?

There is something more "God said let the earth bring forth grass, the herb yielding seed and the tree yielding fruit after his kind, whose seed is in itself". And the earth brought forth grass, One. The herb yielding seed, Two. The tree yielding fruit, Three. There you have the "three" again of resurrection. And the whole of creation became covered with a wonderful growth. A perfect type of resurrection!

Now the Lord Jesus Christ talked about many "three days" as you know. He talked about rising on the third day. "As Jonah was *three* days and *three* nights in the fish's belly, so will the Lord be *three* days and *three* nights in the heart of the earth." "I will destroy this temple and in three days I will raise it again". "He arose the third day according to the scriptures".

## THE EIGHTH

The next day that is important for resurrection is the eighth day. Turn over to John's gospel and you will find that John records this very carefully. And he talks "eight days again". That of course is the first day of the week the day after the seventh; the eighth day. You will find that in the twentieth chapter of John's gospel and verse twenty-six: "And after eight days again".

Eight of course is typical of resurrection. You will remember that eight people were saved in the Ark. That is a perfect type of resurrection. It went under the flood. It landed its crew safe in a new heaven and in a new earth. It is a type of resurrection. Noah is called the *eighth* person.

Something more. If you study the scriptures you will find apart from the Lord Jesus, that there were just eight people resurrected in the Word of God. Just eight!

I will go farther. In our Lord's ministry there were three people resurrected. Those three people in our Lord's ministry are a perfect representation of the three people in the Old Testament that were resurrected. Let us look at them. The first person we read who was raised from the dead in the Old Testament was the son of the widow of Zarephath in I Kings chapter seventeen verses seventeen to twenty-four. The son of a widow.

The Lord Jesus Christ walked along the roads one day and He saw a widow following her son's coffin. And He stopped the funeral procession and He raised the widow's son. A perfect parallel to the raising of the widow's son by Elijah at Zarephath.

The next person that was raised in the Old Testament was the child of a rich person. The son of the woman at Shunam. She was a rich woman. You find that in II Kings four and verses thirty-two to thirty-seven.

The Lord Jesus Christ raised from the dead the child of a rich man, Jarius' daughter.

The last person in the Old Testament that was raised from the dead was in II Kings thirteen and verses twenty to twenty-one. It was a full grown man. After he was buried they put him into the grave of Elijah. And when he touched Elijah's bones he rose from the dead.

And the last person in the New Testament that the Lord Jesus Christ raised from the dead was a full grown man already buried. Lazarus! He was raised from the dead.

So there are six and there are two in the Acts of the Apostles. There were eight people altogether raised from the dead. Eight is the number of resurrection.

What is more, circumcision is a type of resurrection. It is the putting away of the filthiness of the flesh. It was done on the eighth day. And the firstborn son was always given to Jehovah on the eighth day: Exodus twenty-two and verse twenty-nine to thirty. So number eight is a day very significant in the resurrection.

Now having said that I want you to keep these numbers in mind as we come now to this special subject of our Lord's grave clothes.

I want to talk about the *details* of His grave clothes.

I want to talk about the *discarding* of His grave clothes, and I want to talk about the *declaration* of His grave clothes.

**First of all,** *the details*

Come with me to John nineteen and verse thirty-eight and here see three things. One, a new character is introduced; Joseph. Secondly, and old character is reintroduced; Nicodemus. And thirdly, the unique story of our Lord's funeral is told.

The first male person who ever touched the body of the baby Jesus at His birth was Joseph. The last male person to touch the body of the Lord Jesus Christ after His death was another Joseph.

The word Joseph is significant for it means fruitfulness or addition. It is a word significant of resurrection. And it is no coincidence that the first male person to touch our Lord's body was Joseph. And the last person to touch Him after He was dead was another Joseph.

## ARIMATHAEA

Arimathaea in the New Testament is Ramah of the Old Testament. It is the place where Samuel dwelt. Do you remember the story of Samuel? Samuel went to seek a King and he went to Bethlehem. And Jesse landed the whole seven sons up before him. And he said "One of these surely is the Lord's anointed". And the Lord said "No, none of these". And what happened? And Samuel said "Have you no son besides these?" And old Jesse said "Yes, there is an eighth son". (Eight is the number of resurrection as we have seen!) "Go and find him". And when they brought him in, he was filled with the joy of living, his countenance was ruddy. He had come from the full vigour of the field. And the Lord said of David, the eighth son of Jesse, "Arise and anoint him for he shall be King over Israel".

Is it not significant that the man who sought out David, the eighth son, to be the conqueror of Goliath, came from the same city as the man who anointed the Lord for His burial. It was not man that wrote this Book, it was God that wrote it. And every type is fully typified in the New Testament.

## JOSEPH OF ARIMATHAEA

There are some things about Joseph of Arimathaea that you should note. He was a rich man. "He made His grave with the wicked and with the rich in His death". A perfect fulfilment of Isaiah fifty-three! He was an honourable councillor. He waited for the Kingdom of God and he was a disciple of Jesus. But he was a secret disciple. Then what happened? After Jesus died, he went boldly to claim the body of Christ.

Nicodemus was a secret disciple as well. But after the Lord died, he did not come by night to anoint him. He came in the full blaze of day to identify himself with Joseph at His burial. They had looked upon the wounds of Jesus, and looking upon the wounds of Jesus had changed them completely. They are a type of the Jewish nation who one day "shall look on the One whom they have pierced and they shall mourn for Him as one mourneth for his only son". Read the prophecy of Zechariah. This is a type of what is going to happen to the whole Jewish nation when Jesus comes again. The scriptures will be fulfilled.

## NICODEMUS

Let us look at Nicodemus. Is it not interesting that only three times you read about Nicodemus. Of course three is the number of resurrection. It all fits in perfectly together.

You read about Nicodemus in John's gospel chapter three. We all know the passage well, when he came to Jesus by night. But if you turn over to John's gospel chapter seven you read about him again. It says "(he that came to Jesus by night, being one of them.) Doth our law judge any man, before it hear him, and know what he doeth". That is the second reference.

The third reference is at His burial. So you have "three" in connection with Nicodemus.

## THE GRAVECLOTHES THEMSELVES

Now let us look a little more carefully at the graveclothes of the Saviour. They wrapped Him in linen. And if you look at the other scriptures you will find it was *clean* linen, and you will find it was *fine* linen. *Clean* linen and *fine* linen.

When the high priest went within the veil, after the blood had been shed he laid aside his robes of glory and he dressed only in *fine* linen.

Our Lord, our Great High Priest, has now entered within the veil His Blood has been shed, and they wrapped His body in *fine* linen.

They brought also myrrh and aloes. There was myrrh at His birth and there was myrrh at His burial. Frankincense and myrrh were what the wise men brought to Jesus at His birth. Now we have myrrh again at His death. But the Psalmist said that all His garments smell of myrrh and aloes and cassia.

If you turn back to the forty-fifth Psalm you will find in that portion of scripture we have a beautiful story of the Lord Jesus Christ, the great King. And it says "All thy garments smell of myrrh, and aloes, and cassia, out of the ivory palaces" (verse eight). And they anointed Him with myrrh and aloes.

Our Lord at His birth had myrrh brought to Him. He was anointed with spikenard very precious. Mary of Bethany, the sister of Martha, was the one that anointed Him. It was the usual thing to anoint the dead. But there is no suggestion that Lazarus was anointed; because, I believe when the two sisters laid Lazarus in the grave they had faith to believe that Jesus was going to do something for him. And I believe that the spikenard that Mary used had been laid up for her brother's burial and never had been used. But she used it upon the Lord, for the Lord said "She has anointed me for my burial". (You can study that for yourself).

The Lord here is anointed and He is anointed with myrrh and aloes.

Go back to the Old Testament. There has been judgment upon the world. And what does it say? It says after the sacrifice of Noah on Mount Ararat: "the Lord smelled a sweet savour". And we read that the Lord's Sacrifice is a sweet smelling savour to God.

They laid out His body that bore the marks of wounding in His hands, and in His feet and in His side, and upon His back and they anointed it with these sweet smelling spices. These were laid upon the body first, the Jews smeared the body profusely with these ointments, and then they took the sheet and wrapped the sheet round and round and round. The word is "bind". They bound Him in a linen sheet. It is the same thought "she wrapped Him in swaddling clothes and laid Him in a manger". They bound Him. And then they tied around His head the napkin. And they carried Him to a new tomb in which never man was laid. He was virgin born at birth. He was laid in a virgin tomb. Never had a dead body been in that tomb before.

There is one question which will give you the key to what we will be looking at as we continue these studies: Why was it when John went down into the tomb after Peter he believed? John went into the tomb and he saw and believed. I would suggest to you that there is a miracle about the graveclothes. Have a good look at them. Find where the miracle is. And it was the impact of that miracle that made John believe.

Could we come back to what Jesus says a special blessing for everyone of us and what is it? "Blessed are ye that have not seen and yet have believed". Amen and Amen.

# 10 The disdained garments *of Christ*

**I WANT TO CONTINUE** the messages that we have been giving on The Discarded Garments of Christ.

We have looked at His Distinctive Garments. We have paid particular attention to His Distinguished Garments. We have looked at His Disdained Garments and now we are looking at His Discarded Garments.

On four occasions the Lord discarded His garments.

First of all they were discarded for service when He girded Himself with the towel at the passover supper. They were discarded for suffering when they were taken from Him in Pilate's judgment hall, and when He was lashed with the Roman scourge.

They were discarded for sacrifice at Calvary when He was stripped naked and hung upon the accursed tree.

We are going back to the tomb and we are going to see His graveclothes discarded for Sovereignty, for His humiliation has given place to exaltation. His death has given place to endless life, His crucifixion has culminated in His glorious Coronation, and the highest place that heaven affords is His by sovereign right.

Three things about the discarding of His garments for Sovereignty.

First of all the details of His burial. We looked at that in our previous message, and we found things worthy of attention.

We have the introduction of a new person - Joseph of Arimathaea. Then we have the re-introduction of another personality - Nichodemus who visited the Lord by night.

Then we are going on to look at the description of our Lord's unparalleled funeral.

**FULFILMENT**

You know at the cross, and indeed during our Lord's life, prophecy stood guard as a sentinel to ensure that all should be fulfilled. Humanly speaking, at the cross, it seemed impossible that the prophetic scriptures should be fulfilled. Why, there were three prophectic scriptures that seemed humanly impossible to be fulfilled. Number one, that our Lord's bones would not be broken. For it was the custom of the Roman authorities in order to speed the death of the victims on the cross, to break their legs, and that was done with evey victim without exception. The Bible said, "Not a bone of His shall be broken". You might like to check with me that particular scripture. Turn to Psalm thirty-four and verse twenty, in that Messianic Psalm it is made clear: "He keepeth all his bones: not one of them is broken". And of course that is in the fulfilment of a beautiful type of the Lord.

Turn to the book of Exodus and in chapter twelve you have the condition of the Passover Lamb, and the details for its preparation. It is made clear in verse forty-six that no bone of that Lamb should be broken. "In one house shall it be eaten: thou shalt not carry forth ought of the flesh abroad out of the house; neither shall ye break a bone thereof". So away back in Egypt God gave a beautiful type of His Son.

You say to me, "Preacher, have you any scripture for saying that the Passover Lamb is a type of the sacrifice of Christ?" Of course I have. Turn to I Corinthians five and verse seven, and it says, "For even Christ our Passover is sacrificed for us." So Christ is our Passover.

Not a bone of that Passover Lamb was to be broken. The Messianic Psalm said what? "He keepth all his bones, not one of them is broken."

The Lord is hanging on the cross, and the Roman soldiers come and they carry the crowbar between them. They come to the first victim and swing the crowbar against his legs and they are broken. And then they come to Christ. Humanly speaking it seemed that scripture was going to be broken. But prophecy stands as a sentinel guarding Christ even in His death. And when they came to the Lord He was dead already. So they did not break His bones. This is the first scripture.

The second scripture is this. Zechariah chapter twelve and verse ten: "they shall look upon me whom they have pierced". But there was no piercing at the cross. But do you not see that when His legs were not broken the Roman soldier in his hanger, seeing that he could not break His bones because He was dead already, put the spear into the Saviour's side. And if you check in John's gospel chapter nineteen and verse thirty-seven it says "And again another scripture saith, They shall look on Him whom they pierced".

It was the custom of the Romans that when a victim died upon the cross, the body of the victim was buried in a felon's grave. And all those three bodies, humanly speaking, should have been taken down from the cross and buried in a common grave. But the prophet Isaiah said "He made His grave with the wicked, and with the rich in His death". The word "grave" there has not the sense of a burying place but of the act of dying.

"He made His act of dying with the wicked". And on either side of Him upon the cross there were two wicked men. "And with the rich in His death". For when He died they buried Him in a rich man's tomb. So the scriptures were completely and absolutely fulfilled. Let me tell you friend that every prophecy in this Book will be fulfilled.

## THE RESURRECTION

There is another prophecy in this Book which should rejoice the saints of God. It says that some day a trumpet shall sound that shall stir the dark regions of the tomb. And thank God "those that died in Christ shall rise first, and then we that are alive shall be caught up together with them to meet the Lord in the air, and so shall we ever be with the Lord". It will be fulfilled. Yes! All shall be fulfilled!

We find that the prophecies were fulfilled. And one of the men destined by God to fulfil the prophecy was Joseph of Arimathaea. And according to Luke's gospel it was Joseph of Arimathaea who took down the body of our Lord from the cross. That is very interesting.

"Our Lord bore our sins up on His own body on the tree" says Peter. And during the days of Christ's humiliation the hands of wicked men defaced the body of Christ. It was wicked men who scourged Him. It was wicked men who pulled the hairs from off His cheeks. It was wicked hands who crowned Him with thorns and battered and bruised Him in Pilate's judgment hall. It was wicked hands who drove in the nails at the cross. It was a wicked hand which pierced His side. But now that a Fountain had been opened up in the house of David for sin and all uncleanness, no longer did God allow wicked hands to touch the precious body of Christ. And after this it is only the hands of the redeemed that handle the precious body of the Lord. The hands of Joseph, a believer, take the body down from the cross.

There is a carefully given description of what happens. Let me read it to you in John chapter nineteen and verse thirty-nine. It says: "There came also Nicodemus, which at the first came to Jesus by night, and brought a mixture of myrrh and aloes, about an hundred pound weight. Then took they the body of Jesus, and wound it in linen clothes with the spices as the manner of the Jews is to bury".

Turn for a moment to the forty-fifth Psalm and in verse eight it says: "All thy garments smell of myrrh", I want you to notice that the first sweet smelling perfume that is mentioned in this Psalm forty-five is myrrh.

## THE GIFTS

Turn over to Matthew's gospel chapter two. You will find that the wise men when they came to the Lord Jesus offered gifts; gold and frankincense and myrrh, verse eleven of Matthew two. I want you to notice the order. When they came to the Lord when He was born, they offered gold. God is a type of Deity. That gold speaks to me of the pre-existence of Christ from all eternity. Frankincense speaks of the beauty of His life on earth. How beautiful is the life of the Lord Jesus Christ on earth, from Bethlehem to Calvary. But myrrh speaks to me of the sweet savour of His death. When Nicodemus comes you will notice that myrrh takes precedence over the other spices of aloes. And if you go back to the Psalm forty-five you will find "all His garments smell of myrrh" because the sweetest savour of Christ to His people is the savour of His death. His Death is tremendous! His life on earth is wonderful! But without His death upon the cross, without His anointing with myrrh we would not be saved. So the first scent that comes to the believer of the garments of Christ is the sweet savour of His death. Wonderful Jesus! He has garments that are wondrous rare!

I want you to notice that it was linen He was wrapped in. This takes us back to the swaddling clothes. The first garment that wrapped His body was the linen of swaddling clothes. The last garment that He wore before the cross was the linen. (Do you remember I explained to you the five garments of the Galilean peasant - The headdress, the outer coat, the girdle, the sandals, and then the inner vestment which was linen. The inside garment of the Galilean peasant as the outside garment of the priest. What the priest wore on the outside, the peasant wore on the inside). So the last garment in which the Lord appeared before His crucifying, when they stripped Him of His garments was a linen garment as the Priest.

If you read the Old Testament about the robes of the priest you will find that when he entered within the veil, he had to leave aside all the garments of glory and beauty and the only garment that he could wear was the garment of fine linen that was clean.

Turn back to Matthew, Mark and Luke and compare their record with the record of John, you will find that the garment that Jesus wore in the grave was a garment of clean and fine linen, the very material that was directed for the priest when he went within the veil.

I want you to underline the word "wound". They wound it around the body of Christ. When the body was anointed with the aloes and the myrrh they then wrapped the shroud around it. And when the shroud was wrapped around with the spices, the shroud stuck to both the body and to itself. It became a solid, firm garment almost as if the whole body was embalmed.

## THE MIRACLE

I was looking very carefully at this scripture and I was studying very carefully how the Lord was laid to rest, and I came across a very interesting thing. It would be impossible to unwind a body so prepared with these spices after they had settled. It would be impossible to unwind that body without tearing the linen. And then I wondered about a man who came from the dead. A man called Lazarus. And when he came forth from the tomb, do you remember the Lord said "Loose him and let him go". But if Lazarus had been anointed it would have been almost an impossible task to have loosed him to have let him go, because that anointing, the settling of the spices would have been so strong that it would have been a terrible job to loose Lazarus. But Lazarus was not anointed for his burial.

Turn over to the eleventh chapter of John's gospel and verse thirty-nine. What did Martha say when Jesus said "Take ye away the stone". Martha the sister of him that was dead, saith unto Him, "Lord, by this time he stinketh: for he hath been dead four days". If he had been anointed with the powerful spices with which the Jews anointed their dead for burial, he would not have been stinking in four days. For the power of this anointing was so tremendous, that it lasted in the tomb for many, many days. But Mary and Martha laid their brother to rest in faith. They believed that the Lord was coming and the Lord was going to do something. And I will tell you something more, it was not because they had not the money to buy the spices to anoint their brother's body. Turn to chapter twelve and you will find that Mary had the ointment in the house, John chapter twelve and verse three: "Then took Mary a pound of ointment of spikenard, very costly, and anointed the feet of Jesus, and wiped His feet with her hair, and the house was filled with the odour of the ointment". What did Jesus say about it? Verse seven: "Let her alone: against the day of my burying hath she kept this".

Lazarus did not need to be anointed for death for he was to rise by the power of the Saviour's hand. But Christ must enter into all the situations of His people. He was anointed for the death.

Two women watched the funeral. Two Marys watched Joseph of Arimathaea and Nicodemus lay the body of Christ, wound around, bound in the linen with the napkin around his head in a tomb where never man was laid, for the virgin Christ who was born of a virgin mother must lie in a virgin tomb. And the stone was rolled to the door and our Lord was buried.

**DISCARDED**

We come now to the discarding of His garments. Turn over to the twentieth chapter of John and verse one: "The first day of the week cometh Mary Magdalene early, when it was yet dark, unto the sepulchre, and seeth the stone taken away from the sepulchre". And she ran to get Simon Peter and John and told them. And Simon Peter and John ran to the sepulchre John, of course, was only a boy of seventeen years of age or so at this time. Peter must have been a man of over forty years of age. So the young boy outstripped the older man and came to the sepulchre first. In the verse four of John twenty it says "So they ran both together, and the other disciple did out run Peter, and came first to the sepulchre. And he stooping down, and looking in, saw the linen clothes lying; yet went he not in". The words that are used in the Greek text in that particular verse are the words that are used for glancing. He simply stooped down and took a glance in, and he saw the linen clothes lying. "Then cometh Simon Peter following him, and went into the sepulchre, and seeth the linen clothes lie". (verse six)

That seeing is different from looking in. That is inspecting or scrutinising. So Peter scrutinised. John looked in with a glance. Peter inspected what had taken place. "And the napkin, that was about His head not lying with the linen clothes, but wrapped together in a place by itself". Then went in also that other disciple, which came first to the sepulchre, and he saw, and believed". (verses seven, eight) That word "saw" is another different word. And that word is not "glancing or "inspecting". That word is perceiving and understanding. "He saw and believed". What does that mean?

## WRAPPED TOGETHER

The whole secret of this matter is found in the words "wrapped together". You see our Lord was bound. He was bound with the linen, and about the head with a napkin. If His friends had come to take Him away they would not have attempted to tear up the linen clothes because that would have been an impossibility. They would have taken Him with the clothes around Him, if a friend had done that. If an enemy had done it, they would have done the very same thing. But the word there "wrapped together means that the garment, the napkin, the linen clothes lying, they were in the actual shape in which they were bound around the Lord. The Lord did not rise and take them off. The Lord rose through the graveclothes. And could I say this, the angel did not come down from heaven and let the Lord out. The stone was rolled away to let you in to see that the Lord was already out. Let us get that perfectly clear. In just the same way as the Lord went through the doors of the upper room where the disciples were, He went through the rock face. But He also went through the graveclothes. And if you had gone into that tomb you would have seen the very shape of the Lord's body impressed on those clothes.

When we lie down to die, the shape of the Lord's body is imprinted on the believer's death. Dear believer, you will lie in the place where Jesus lay. And when you lie down to die you will lie down with this blessed hope "As my Lord rose so will I rise again".

What happened? There was a miracle. And John saw the miracle. That is why he believed. He did not believe because he simply saw the graveclothes. It was the shape and the manner of the graveclothes, with the napkin about the Lord's head lying in a place by itself, where the head would lie, and the rest of the clothes in the place where they would lie around His body. "And he believed". He believed! And what a wonderful belief that was. It swelled up in the heart of John.

## JOSEPH

You know the Lord Jesus Christ is typified in the Old Testament. He is typified by a man called Joseph. Joseph is a beautiful type of Christ. Joseph was the beloved son of the father. So Jesus is the Beloved Son of the Father. Joseph was given the special robe. So Christ is robed in the garment of beauty. And God has said "Let all the angels of God worship Him".

You know Joseph was condemned, and so was the Lord. Joseph had two companions; the butler and the baker. One of his companions was saved, and one of them was lost. Christ was in the place of condemnation and He had two companions. Two dying thieves. One was saved and one was lost. Joseph did not remain forever in the place of condemnation. For the king sent for him and he went from the prison to the king's palace. My Lord did not remain forever in the tomb. Thank God, He is on the Throne. But if you go back to Genesis chapter forty-one and verse fourteen you read this; before Joseph left the prison he changed his garments. Before he left the prison he changed his garments. He left aside the old prison rags. And thank God the rags of death have been left aside forever. My Lord sits KING OF KINGS, AND LORD OF LORDS. And He says to His people "I have conquered death and hell for you. And I have the keys of death and hell at my girdle".

Do you think He will ever lock one of His saints in the prison house of death forever, or into hell forever? My Saviour bears the keys. And you know instead of locking us in, praise God He has locked Hell's door against me forever.

No one will ever open it for me, for my Saviour has got the keys. This is the declaration of these clothes. Christ slipped out of death's clutches and so will I. This vile body is going to be changed in a moment, in the twinkling of an eye, at the last trump. When the mortal body shall put on immortality. When this corruptible shall put on incorruptible. And then shall be brought about the saying "O death, where is thy sting, O grave, where is thy victory?"

No wonder angels came down to celebrate. No wonder angels will celebrate the rising again of the people of God.

Go into the tomb today.

"Let me like Mary through the gloom, Come with a gift for Thee, Show to me now the empty tomb, Lead me to Calvary, Lest I forget Gethsemane, Lest I forget Thine agony, Lest I forget Thy love to me, Lead me to Calvary."

# 11 The crown *of thorns*

**"AND WHEN THEY HAD** platted a crown of thorns, they put it upon his head, and a reed in his right hand: and they bowed the knee before him, and mocked him, saying, Hail, King of the Jews!" - Matthew twenty-seven verse twenty-nine.

I want to consider with you a subject of the deepest solemnity. I want to speak of, and I want you to meditate upon the crown of thorns that Jesus wore.

Just before we enter into the common hall of Pilate, the Roman governor, to see the Lord Jesus Christ, I want to pause on the threshold of the doorway for a quiet moment of meditation. I want you to think for a moment of the One Who is here brought down to the deepest shame. I want to contemplate His *Person* and I want to consider His *Power*.

Who is this Person set at nought in Pilate's judgment hall? Who is the One of whom Pilate says, "Behold the Man?" Who is this Prisoner subjected to all the shame and all the ignominy of the scourging and mockery of the Praetorium? Who is He?

I want you to remember the excellency of His Person. I want you to remember the glory of His Eternal Majesty. I want you to remember that this is God's Incarnate Son - the One whom angels dared not look upon in eternity but rather veiled their faces and cried "Holy! Holy! Holy! Lord God Almighty". This One is the Everlasting Son Who was in the bosom of the Everlasting Father. He is the One of whom the Father said at His Incarnation "Let all the angels of God worship Him".

Here is God of gods, Light of lights, Very God of very God and Very man of very man. But now He is put to shame. Remember His Person as we continue to meditate on the crown of thorns.

I want you to remember something else equally important if you are going to get this tremendous theme into its proper perspective. I want you to think upon His Power. He is the One Who threw the stars out into the heavens. He is the One Who spread the blue curtains of the universe around. He is the One who set the stars in their courses. He is the One Who created all things by the Word of His Power. He is the One Who keeps this old world going, for "by Him all things consist". He is the consistency which keeps nature together and keeps it moving in its pre-ordained, pre-ordered way. In His hand is all the strength of heaven. In His breast heaves all the power of eternity. Yet this is the One, the All powerful One, the Eternal God enthroned in humanity, who is set at nought by the soldiers in the Praetorium.

Having thus considered the Person and Power of the Blessed Christ of God, we cross over the threshold of the hall and fix our gaze on the crown of thorns which is so cruelly fixed upon His lovely brow. We are going to direct our meditation particularly to this garland of thorns. There are seven things about the crown to which I want to pay attention.

First of all I want to speak of the *material* of the crown, it was a crown of thorns. We must look at the significance of the thorns.

Secondly, I want to draw your attention to the *making* of the crown. They platted a crown of thorns and put it upon His head.

Thirdly, I will speak of the *misery* of the crown. We want to enter into the Holiest of All and have fellowship with Christ in His sufferings and see something of the depths of misery which the Son of God experienced when he was crowned with thorns. We want to watch these soldiers as they take the reed and beat that cruel crown into the temples of the fair head of our lovely Lord.

Fourthly, I must call attention to the *mockery* of the crown. Oh the depths of the ridicule which Christ waded through as He made His way to dark Calvary! You will notice that over and over again it is recorded by the divine penman that the soldiers mocked Him - "they mocked Him" ... "they mocked Him".

Fifthly, I will come to the very heart of this sublime subject and ponder with you the *meaning* of the crown. That crown has a tremendous meaning. The meaning of the crown will introduce my sixth point - the *mystery* of the crown. For there's mystery, deep mystery here.

Finally, I want to conclude with the *message* of the crown.

## I. THE MATERIAL OF THE CROWN

"A crown of *thorns*". The material for the construction of this crown was thorns.

Now let me emphasise this fact, that when the world came from the hand of the Creator there was not a thorn on any plant upon its surface, nor the seed of thorn in any part of its soil. Thorns were no part of the perfect earth over which heaven announced its approval "All very good". At that time the rose bloomed without thorns and the berries were brought forth without briars. It was a thornless world which God had created. Thorns, let me emphasise, are the result of sin. Thorns are the natural fruit of sin.

People come along and they say "Why does this happen?" Tragedies happen because men have sinned. Do you know why there are thorns in this world? Because you are a sinner. Do you know why you are having a thorn in your heart? Do you know why you are having a thorny experience and you are among the briars? I will tell you why. It is because you have sinned and gone astray from God.

Turn over in your Bible to Genesis, chapter three and let us note carefully verses seventeen and eighteen. Remember, God is the speaker.

"And unto Adam he said, Because thou hast hearkened unto the voice of thy wife, and hast eaten of the tree of which I commanded thee, saying, Thou shalt not eat of it: cursed is the ground for thy sake; in sorrow shalt thou eat of it all the days of thy life; Thorns also and thistles shall it bring forth to thee; and thou shalt eat the herb of the field".

The fall has come. Man has plunged into the abyss of sin, and the world with Adam has sunk in the abyss of iniquity. By one man sin has entered into the world, and death by sin. God meets fallen man in Eden's garden and the curse of sin is set forth and thus we have the origin of the thorn. Are you beginning to see the significance of the material from which the crown was made? They had no trouble getting thorns, for there are thorns everywhere and the Rabbis of Israel recorded that there were twenty-five kinds of thorns in the Holy Land.

You know when God created this earth of ours there were roses without thorns and berries without briars, but when man fell there never was another rose without a thorn nor another berry without a briar. Thorns are the proof of sin. Briars are the insignia of the fall.

## II. THE MAKING OF THE CROWN

"they platted a crown of thorns"

This crown of thorns was made by the hands of men. The "they" in our text refers to the whole band of soldiers. They were all united in making this crown of thorns. They had one thought, one objective, one goal in mind. We'll make a "crown of thorns", that is what every heart proposed.

Now it would have been impossible to make a crown of thorns without pricking your fingers. Yes, and the long eastern thorn of Palestine is very, very sharp, and apt to pierce and draw blood. Do you know that as they made this crown of thorns they themselves were identified with the making, and upon it was their own blood? I want you to get this. Before the blood of Jesus dyed those thorns, they were already stained by its makers. The blood is the life and Christ answered blood for blood and a life for a life in His great atoning sacrifice on Calvary.

Could I also draw another lesson here? If you, sinner, play with sin it will really prick you and wound you and rob you of your very life. The price of sin is your life's blood. No one ever played with sin and got away with it. Sin always demands blood for blood and life for life. If you think you can plait the thorns of sin and lie down in the briars of iniquity and get away with it you are only a fool. Sin, when it is finished, will leave you scarred and marked and broken and pricked to the eternal death. How often this happens. Are you playing with the thorns of sin? Are you occupied in plaiting a crown of thorns to place on the head of Jesus? Remember, to plait a crown of thorns for Jesus in time is to make a bed of thorns for your own souls for all eternity.

**III. THE MISERY OF THE CROWN**

"and put it on His head"

The crown is made. The Lord Jesus Christ is set up onto a chair in imitation of a throne. They strip Him stark naked. Yes, He despised the shame. The holy, sinless, harmless, all-lovely Son of God and Son of man, was stripped in Pilate's judgment hall. After the cruel scourging by which they ploughed His quivering back with stripes, they threw over his shoulders a purple and scarlet robe in mockery of royalty. Then they take the crown of thorns and in mockery of a coronation, they place it upon His head. You can see the cruelty of the soldier who does the vile deed as he plants, with all his power, the jagged chaplet on the temples of Jesus. I hope you are getting this, that the Lord Jesus Christ is now bearing your curse.

There was a day in the earth when God had to plant a thorn because of the curse. There came another day, however, when God planted my curse on the head of my Substitute. His very Own Blessed Son.

I want you to think of the misery which Jesus now endures. His temples are penetrated with the long eastern thorns. From every penetration and laceration there runs a river of blood right down His lovely face.

I want you to see Him. The sacred head is now wounded. The Son of God has had His coronation not with a crown of diadems, but with a crown of thorns. We want to gaze upon His misery.

The misery inflicted by this crown of anguish is twofold. It is both *outward* and *inward*. Let us consider first, the outward agony of wearing this crown.

What agony upon the temple! What pangs of pain in the head! Remember the sensitivity of the head to pain. Yes, and not content with the mere crowning, the soldiers take a reed and they start to hammer His blessed head with it. So they drive the thorns right down into His head. They seek to plunge Him into the very depths of anguish. Before they mock Him, they lead Him through the vale of the darkest misery. I hear the quick drawing of His breath as the thorns penetrate His temples. Oh the misery of the crown of thorns!

Let us never forget that this outward misery is not to be compared to the inward misery of the God-man.

You know He was born to be King. Upon His temple should have been a crown of diamonds. Upon His temple should have been a crown unparalleled amongst the crowns of the world. He should have been crowned with many crowns, for He was the Prince of the kings of the earth. I wonder how He felt in His human soul as men crowned Him with thorns? He knew He was the King of Kings, and yet, behold, He is crowned with thorns. He knew He was born to be King. He knew that His was a royalty without rival amongst the sons of men, and yet into the depths of misery He must sink. He didn't draw back. He could have seized that reed with the strength of omnipotence. He could have smitten every soldier in the Praetorium. He could have caused the pavement of the hall to cleave in twain and hurled them like Korah, Dathan and Abiram of old, alive into Tophet.

But no, He bears it willingly, He bears it patiently., He bears it meekly. He despises the shame as He is crowned with thorns. Oh the inward misery of God's

Son! A crown of agony was on His temples; yes, but a forest of briars was in His heart.

## IV. THE MOCKERY OF THE CROWN

What terrible mockery Christ is subjected to at this particular time in His Passion. Jesus was born King of the Jews. You remember the wise men came seeking for the One "born King of the Jews".

He came from the greatest throne, the throne of the God of heaven. His Father gave Him as mediator, the Kingship and Headship over all things to the Church.

King Jesus was His name. Here, in Pilate's hall, the blasphemous legionaires mocked His Kingship and ridiculed His Kingdom. Notice the steps in this mockery.

First of all they *repudiate His Claims*

This they did by crowning Him with thorns. "You are a King, are you?" They jeeringly challenged. "You're the King of the Jews, are you not? We'll crown you King! We'll show you what we think of you. See this crown of thorns. We'll make this your coronation day. We'll crown you and then we'll do homage to you".

So they do their nefarious work of crowning God's Son with thorns. Kneeling before Him in mock homage, they sneeringly cried, "Hail, King of the Jews". Then, rising to their feet, they buffet His tender face, pull out the hairs of His beard and spit upon Him. Thus they repudiate His claims.

Secondly, *they ridiculed His Character*

They sought in every way to ridicule the spotless, sinless character of my precious Lord. The Lord Jesus prophesied not only of His crucifixion, but of His scourging. This, of course forms part of the scourging, the ridiculing of His Character. This is the prelude to the depths of the anguish of the Cross. The overtures of my Saviour's death-knell are being sounded in the Roman Praetorium. Down the corridor of mocking, the Lord Jesus passes to the cross. Yes, and as He passes down they ridicule His character.

Thirdly, *they rejected His Compassion*

As He sat despised and rejected, upon His countenance was infinite compassion. Alas, not one of the soldiers accepted His love. They all rejected His Compassion. As the blood flowed from His temples; as the spittles mingled with that blood; as man's spittles and God's blood intermingled together, His eyes beamed heavenly compassion on His assaulters. So hardened, so callous and so brutal were those sinners that they mocked Him more and more by rejecting His Compassion.

Thus, you have mocked Him. O mockers of the lowly Jesus beware, lest you come to that loathsome place where God shall mock you.

Fourthly, *they refused His Commandments*

These soldiers knew well Who Jesus was and what His message was. The teaching of the Prophet of Nazareth has resounded from Galilee in the north to Judea in the south. By crowning Him with thorns they publicly refused His commandments.

I wonder, does this day find *you* a mocker of the Lord Jesus? You, who have repudiated His Claims, you who have ridiculed His Character, you who have rejected His Compassion, you who have refused His Commandments, you are a mocker of Jesus Christ.

Christ claims to be King, and you have rebelled against His sceptre and refused His throne its regal rights. Yes, and you have ridiculed His Character. What of that foul blasphemy which your lips uttered? What of that evil in your heart directed against His holy person. Further, you have rejected His

Compassion. You have abused gospel opportunity after gospel opportunity and turned your back on the redeeming love of the Saviour. Yet again you have refused His Commandment. "And this is His commandment, that we should believe in the name of His Son Jesus Christ".

## V. THE MEANING OF THE CROWN

Now the thorns speak of *the curse*. That's one thing that they speak of. The thorns also speak of the world. Do you remember the parable of the sower? Let me turn you to two verses -

"And some fell among thorns; and the thorns sprung up, and choked them: He also that received seed among the thorns is he that heareth the word; and the care of this world, and the deceitfulness of riches, choke the word, and he becometh unfruitful." (Matthew thirteen verses seven and twenty two.)

So the thorns represent *the world*.

Now turn over to Numbers thirty-three and verse fifty-five and you will find that the nations that Israel failed to drive out from Canaan are likened unto them. These nations are typical of the flesh. So the thorns represent *the flesh*. Now, how did the curse come? It came because Eve paid heed to the devil. *Hence, in the thorns we have a perfect type of the world, the flesh and the devil.*

Now the Lord Jesus is crowned with the thorns which speak to me of the curse. The curse must find a place to rest. It must find an object for its wrath. Someone must suffer. The sentence must be carried out to its last letter.

Praise God, the curse has passed from my head tonight to the head of my Substitute, the Lord of Glory. Hallelujah! Then thousand times Hallelujah, Jesus has borne my curse.

I have to face up to the power of *the devil*, haven't I? What a grip! What tremendous strength the devil has! What terrible power he sways! He maims, he holds, he chains men to his bond-service. The fury of the devil came against my Substitute and the Saviour broke and smashed forever the devil's power over me. My Lord is Victor Emmanuel, the Conqueror of Hell and the Slayer of the old Serpent and Dragon of the Pit. Hear the Word of God.

"Forasmuch then as the children are partakers of flesh and blood, he also himself likewise took part of the same: that through death he might destroy him that had the power of death, that is, the devil; And deliver them who through fear of death were all their lifetime subject to bondage". Hebrews two verses fourteen and fifteen.

The crown represents deliverance from the curse, yes, and deliverance from the devil. That's why you're not saved isn't it? You're held, bound, chained, fettered and imprisoned, but, Praise God, Jesus can break the power of the devil in your life.

Yes, and there's another old enemy in my heart, and the things I would not, those are the very things I do. That enemy is *the flesh*.

The flesh lusteth against the spirit and the spirit against the flesh, and these two are contrary, the one to the other. Is there any victory over me? Can I be delivered from myself? Can I be delivered from my lusts and habits and passions? Hallelujah, there is complete deliverance.

*Christ breaks the power of cancelled sin;*
*He sets the prisoner free.*
*His blood can make the vilest clean;*
*His blood avails for me.*

The power of the flesh has been dealt with in Christ. "For what the law could not do, in that it was weak through the flesh, God sending His own Son in the likeness of sinful flesh and for sin, condemned sin in the flesh: That the righteousness of the law might be fulfilled in us, who walk not after the flesh, but after the Spirit" (Romans eight verses three and four).

*The world* also is a great enemy, and it has many attractions. The world holds forth its hands and offers me its pleasures. It offers me its companionships. It offers me its privileges. It offers me its excitements. Is there any escape from the temptations of the world? Yes, here it is.

"But God forbid that I should glory, save in the cross of our Lord Jesus Christ, by whom the world is crucified unto me, and I unto the world. (Galatians six verse fourteen).

I gaze upon the crown of thorns and I learn its meaning. It spells deliverance from the world, the flesh and the devil, and as I learn this tremendous truth I shout in joyful emancipation, "Hallelujah, and ten thousand times Hallelujah!"

This is the meaning of the crown of thorns. Christ is my Substitute and He is crowned with the result of sin.

I am saved, and as the result of the Crown of Agony I am crowned with everlasting joy.

The old prophet was right you know -

"And the ransomed of the Lord shall return, and come to Zion with songs and everlasting joy upon their heads; they shall obtain joy and gladness, and sorrow and sighing shall flee away". (Isaiah thirty-five verse ten).

Notice its' everlasting joy that's on their head. The curse has changed to blessing, for Christ wore the bitter crown for me.

*The bitter sorrow that He bore,*
*And, oh, the crown of thorns He wore,*
*That I might live for evermore,*
*Is more than tongue can tell*

As we ponder upon the meaning of the crown I think you will perceive that there is mystery, deep mystery here.

## VI. THE MYSTERY OF THE CROWN

Do you know that the crown of thorns is *the fulfilment of a wonderful prophecy?* The Lord of Glory had all these things in prophecy, but we don't see them. We haven't, alas, the spiritual eyesight to see them. When we really ponder the Book we begin to see. "Lord, open Thou mine eyes that I may behold wondrous things out of Thy Word" - that should be our prayer every time we open the Book

Now, the most precious type of the Sacrifice of Jesus is found in Genesis, chapter twenty-two. In this chapter you will find that the Lord commanded Abraham to offer his only son upon the altar. He was to offer him on the Mount

Moriah, that's the same mount as the Mount Calvary - the very place where Jesus was to die. This is a tremendous type. Remember, his only son, Isaac, was laid upon the altar and Abraham took the knife to slay him. Then came the Divine intervention.

"And the angel of the Lord called unto Him out of heaven, and said, Abraham, Abraham: and he said Here am I. And he said, Lay not thine hand upon the lad, neither do thou any thing unto him: for now I know that thou fearest God, seeing thou hast not withheld thy son, thine only son from me. And Abraham lifted up his eyes, and looked, and behold behind him a ram caught in a thicket by his horns and Abraham went and took the ram, and offered him up for a burnt offering in the stead of his son." (Genesis twenty two verses eleven to thirteen).

Do you see it? Abraham took the ram which was caught in the thicket by his horns, and he transferred it to the altar. He then took Isaac from off the altar and Isaac was saved and the ram, caught by its head in the thicket, was offered in the stead of Isaac. Now the word that is used for thicket here is theword used for a thicket of thorns. This is most interesting. Turn to Isaiah nine verse eighteen "For wickedness burneth as the fire: it shall devour the briars and thorns, and shall kindle in the thickets of the forest, and they shall mount up like the lifting smoke". Notice the thorns and briars made up the thicket. Now, away back in the dawning of patriarchal history there was a ram caught by its head in the thorns. A perfect type of the Lord Jesus Christ. No wonder the Saviour Himself could say, "Abraham rejoiced to see my day, and he saw it and was glad" (John eight verse fifty-six). He saw the meaning of substitution and resurrection as he lifted Isaac down from the altar alive. It was all possible because the head of the ram was encircled by thorns which held it fast for the sacrifice.

There is further mystery here. Do you not know that the crown of thorns is *the chaplet of victory?*

When two opponents contended for the victory in the arena, if the champion was defeated, his victor seized his laurel crown and it was placed in triumph upon his own head. The crown of thorns is the crown of the old champion, sin, the insignia of sin's dominion. Praise God, that age-long champion, sin, is defeated forever by our Lord Jesus Christ; and the Almighty Victor Emmanuel seized sin's crown and wears it triumphantly. What man meant to be a gory crown of shame is in reality a glorious crown of victory. Thus Christ robbed sin of its most glorious regalia, and on the field of battle He is crowned eternal champion.

Yes, but there is further mystery here. Do you not know that the crown of thorns is in order to *the blooming of the Rose of Sharon?*

In this accursed earth there cannot be a rose without a thorn. As I gaze on the thorny crown I learn that this is in order that the Rose of Sharon may bloom for me. There can be no rose of heaven's pardon, heaven's peace or heaven's power without those thorns. As I consider the thorns I burst forth into the song

"Sweet Rose of Sharon blooming for me".

The fragrance of that rose fills my soul and I am satisfied with Jesus.

Again, do you not know that the thorns *speak of the security of the children of God?*

You have no doubt noticed how the tiny bird makes its nest right in the centre of the blackthorn hedge with its thousands of prickles. The little bird finds security there, the thorns sheltering it from harm. So I would build my nest for eternity within the thorns of Jesus. It is a safe place for me, the sinner. There no harm can befall me and no fear can be. Job had a hedge planted round him by God. That same God has hedged His people in with the thorns of His Son. The pangs of His Son's passion, that's where I have built my nest forever. Hallelujah!

## VII. THE MESSAGE OF THE CROWN

The message of the crown is two-fold. It speaks of *dark perdition*. You can take the crown of rejection and press it on the temples of the Christ of God. You can crucify to yourself, afresh, the Lord of Glory and put Him to an open shame.

It speaks of *glorious pardon*. You can kneel at Christ's feet, and, realising that He wore sin's cruel crown for you, you can crown Him Lord of All. It's either the crown of perdition or pardon. God grant you will crown Him, the Lamb upon the throne, as your Saviour, Lord and King.

*O Sacred head once wounded,*
*With grief and pain weighed down,*
*How scornfully surrounded*
*With thorns, Thine only crown!*
*How art Thou pale with anguish,*
*With sore abuse and scorn!*
*How does that visage languish,*
*That once was bright as morn.*

*O sacred Head, what glory,*
*What bliss till now was Thine!*
*Yet, though despised and gory,*
*I joy to call Thee mine;*
*Thy grief and Thy compassion*
*Were all for sinners's gain;*
*Mine, mine was the transgression,*
*But Thine the deadly pain.*

*What language shall I borrow*
*To praise Thee, heavenly Friend,*
*For this Thy dying sorrow,*
*Thy pity without end?*
*Lord, make me Thine for ever,*
*Nor let me faithless prove;*
*Oh, let me never, never*
*Abuse such dying love!*

# 12 The many crowns *of Christ*

**FOR SOME TIME WE** have been considering the subject of the Wardrobe of Christ or the Wonderful Garments of our Wonderful Lord.

I thought I would bring to conclusion this series of messages on the Lord's Garments with a message on The Lord's Crowns.

Turn over to Revelation chapter nineteen and verse twelve. Here we read "And on His head were many crowns".

The Lord Jesus Christ is very, very precious to His people. No wonder the spouse in Solomon's Song said "Oh that I knew where I could find Him". And no wonder the apostle Paul, after a quarter of a century witnessing faithfully for the Saviour, could pen the words "That I might know Him".

One of the most interesting studies in scripture is the Person of the Lord Jesus Christ. And everything about the Lord Jesus Christ is fascinating. And everything about Him is instructive.

We have in this text two thoughts. The head that is crowned and the crowns upon the head. Only twice in the Bible is there a description of the Lord's head. Once in the Old Testament and once in the New Testament.

Turn with me to the fifth chapter of Solomon's Song. And here we have a description of the head of Christ. Verse eleven of chapter five. And we read there: "His head is as the most fine gold, His locks are bushy, and black as a raven". Now keep your finger on that scripture and turn over to Revelation chapter on. And here you have another description of the Lord Jesus Christ. Verse fourteen of chapter one of Revelation: "His head and His hairs were white like wool, as white as snow"; There is a great difference between the description in Revelation and the description in Solomon's Song. For the description in Solomon's Son is Christ before the cross. And the description in Revelation is Christ after the cross.

**THE HEAD OF CHRIST**

I might mention that the head is the seat of the mind. It is where the brain is located. The centre of the mind.

The best commentary that I could make upon that description "His head is as the most fine gold" is found over in Philippians chapter two and verses five to eleven. You will find in this chapter the Holy Spirit's commentary on that great statement "His head is as the most fine gold". And you will find that seven things (seven is the number of perfection) are brought out in that passage: "Let this mind be in you, which was also in Christ Jesus". (The head is the centre of the mind)

First, His Deity: "Who, being in the form of God".

Secondly, His Co-equality: "Thought it not robbery to be equal with God".

Thirdly, His Humanity: "But made Himself of no reputation, and took upon Him the form of a servant, and was made in the likeness of men".

Fourthy, His Humility: "and being found in fashion as a man, He humbled Himself".

Fifthly, His Agony: "He became obedient unto death, even the death of the cross".

Sixthly, His Majesty: "Wherefore God also hath highly exalted Him, and given Him a name which is above every name".

Seventhly, His Sovereignty: "That at the Name of Jesus every knee shall bow, of things in heaven, and things in earth, and things under the earth; And that every tongue, should confess that Jesus Christ is Lord, to the glory of God the Father".

But you will notice that in the Song of Solomon "His locks are bushy and black as a raven". I want you to notice that word "His locks". That is very significant! The only men in the Old Testament that had locks were those under the vow of the Nazarite. And if you want to know what the Nazarite's vow was, you will find it in Numbers chapter six and verse five: "All the days of the vow of his separation there shall no razor come upon his head: until the days be fulfilled, in the which he separateth himself unto the Lord, he shall be holy, and shall let the locks of his hair grow". So the person in the Old Testament; the Jewish male had long locks when he was under the law of the Nazarite.

Do you remember it was said of Samson "No razor shall come upon his head, the child shall be a Nazarite unto God from the womb". Compare with Matthew chapter two and verse twenty-three, of Christ it was said "He shall be called a Nazarene". And so Christ had these locks before the cross. Why? Because there was a vow upon Christ. Christ had taken a vow for His people. He vowed! What did He vow? He vowed that He would go to Calvary. And that He would suffer shame upon Calvary. He vowed that He would fulfil, all that He promised His Father to do for His people. So before the cross He is described with the locks in his hair. But there is something else. He is described as "hair that is black as a raven". Notice it! The raven in scripture is an unclean fowl. It was not to be eaten. If you look at Leviticus chapter eleven and thirteen to fifteen: "And these are they which ye shall have in abomination among the fowls; they shall not be eaten, Every raven after his kind". I hope you are getting the significance friend. The raven is an unclean fowl. The Lord's hair is described as a raven. It was a bird of the curse. And on the head of Christ was to come the curse. And those locks were a vow which He took to the Father, that He would undergo the curse for you and me. And one day upon the black locks of my Saviour's head there was set the crown of thorns. And He endured the curse for you and me.

## A CHANGE AND CONTRAST

Now leave that, and turn over to Revelation chapter one. You have a distinct change and a tremendous contrast. Christ has now endured the cross. But the marks of suffering are upon Him forever.

You know when you get to heaven there will be no marks of suffering upon your body. I have got good news for you. All the wrinkles will be taken out! All those parts that you try to cover up, my dear woman, with a little bit of putty or powder or paint will be all taken away. He is going to present us without a spot or wrinkle or any such thing. But there will be a body in heaven that shall bear for all eternity the marks of suffering. It is the body of my Lord. He will have the scars in His hands and His feet, and the scars upon His brow. I know they will be radiated in glory, but His body will bear eternally the marks of the cross. When we get to heaven, His head is not black like the raven, but "His hair and His head (look at it) were white like wool, as white as snow". The only other place in the Bible where wool and snow are likened in simile together is in Isaiah chapter one and verse eighteen. It is to do with the cleansing of God's people; "Come now, and let us reason together, saith the Lord: though your sins be as scarlet, they shall be as white as snow; though they be red like crimson, they shall be as wool". The whiteness is something which man cannot make. It is the whiteness of the snowflake. It is heavenly, it is divine wool. It is the whiteness of the Lamb's coat. It is the whiteness of the sacrifice that is given, His blood for the salvation of the world. And it is upon that head that the crowns today are set.

*"The head that once was crowned with thorns,*
*Is crowned with glory now,*
*A Royal diadem adorns the Mighty Victor's brow".*

Let us turn over to the gospels. And you will notice something if you read the gospels carefully. The first part of His body that the Lord ever referred to in scripture was His head. That was the first part of the body that the Lord ever referred to.

The first part of the Lord's body that is ever mentioned in scripture is His heel. That is over in Genesis chapter three and verse fifteen: "And I will put enmity between Thee and the woman, and between Thy seed and her seed; and it shall bruise thy head, and thou shalt bruise His heel".

The first part of the body that the Lord Himself ever referred to is His head. Turn over to Matthew eight and verse twenty. And this is what the Lord says of His head: "And Jesus saith unto him. The foxes have holes, and the birds of the air have nests; but the Son of Man hath not where to lay His head". The unreclining head of Christ!

I have made a careful study of the head of Christ in the gospels. And I have discovered that there are five direct references to the Lord's head in the gospels.

**FIVE REFERENCES TO CHRIST'S HEAD**

The first one; The unreclining head of Christ, Matthew chapter eight.

Turn over to Matthew chapter twenty-six and verse seven. It says: There came unto Him a woman having an alabaster box of very precious ointment, and poured it on His head, as He sat at meat". The anointed head of Christ!

There were only two parts of the Lord's body ever anointed while He was living. One was His feet. You will find that in Luke seven and verse thirty-eight. The other was His head. The anointed head of Christ.

Let me tell you something. There were people anointed in the Bible. Three types of people were anointed in the Bible. Kings were anointed in the Bible. Priests were anointed in the Bible. Prophets were anointed in the Bible. Jesus Christ is our Anointed Priest, Anointed  Prophet and He is our Anointed King. You will notice that this anointment was to His burying. He showed Himself by His death that He was our Priest, His death that He was our King, and by His death that He was our Prophet. The anointed head of Christ.

Then you have in Matthew twenty-seven and verse twenty-nine, the Battered Head of Christ. The place of His sufferings. "And when they had platted a crown of thorns, they put it upon His head, and a reed in His right hand: and they bowed the knee before Him, and mocked Him, saying, Hail, King of the Jews! And they spit upon Him, and took the reed, and smote Him on the head. They drove the thorns down into His temples. The Battered Head of Christ!

Turn over to John's gospel chapter nineteen. You have the Bowed Head of Christ. John chapter nineteen and verse thirty: "When Jesus therefore had received the vinegar, He said, It is finished: and He bowed His head, and gave up the ghost". The Bowed Head of Christ!

Then in John twenty and verse seven you will find The Wrapped Head of Christ. "And the napkin that was about His head, not lying with the linen clothes, but wrapped together in a place by itself". We dealt with that in our last message. So the very wrapping of His head has a special mention. For His head is of utmost importance.

Time does not permit to deal with the significance of the Unreclining Head of Christ; "He had not where to lay His head".

We have not time to deal with the full significance of the Anointed Head of Christ, or the Battered head of Christ, or the Bowed Head of Christ, or the Wrapped Head of Christ. But let me say this, it is that Head which is now crowned with many crowns.

It is significant in a study of this subject that "five" runs throughout it.

You know God's people can have five crowns. Did you know that? Did you know that you, in heaven, could be given five crowns? There are five crowns for the believer. Let us look at them because they are all related to Christ. And they all bring out some peculiar setting of His Kingship.

James chapter one and verse twelve is the first scripture I would refer you to. James one and verse twelve: "Blessed is the man that endureth temptation: for when he is tried, he shall receive the crown of life, which the Lord hath promised to them that love Him". That is one of the crowns God's people can attain to, "the crown of Life".

Turn over to Revelation chapter two and verse ten. It says: "Fear none of those things which thou shalt suffer: behold the devil shall cast some of you into prison, that ye may be tried; and ye shall have tribulation ten days: be thou faithful unto death, (look at it) and I will give thee a crown of life".

**That is the first crown, a crown of life.**

## THE CROWN OF LIFE

Who could give us a crown of life? Ah! when we compare the scripture we find that the Lord Jesus Christ is a King Who can give us a crown of life. And He is the only One Who can give us a crown of life. What sort of King is He? Turn to I Timothy chapter one and verse seventeen: Here is Christ the King, but He is a special King. He is a King that can give us a crown of life. Why? Look at it: "Now unto the King Eternal, Immortal, Invisible, the only wise God, be honour and glory for ever and ever". He gives the crown of life. He is the Immortal. So the King Eternal can give to me a crown of life.

"On His head were many crowns". He wears the crown of the King Eternal, Immortal, Invisible.

God grant that we will be recipients of the crown of life. It is not only given to the martyr you know. But it is given to the man that endures temptation. Some of us will not be privileged to wear the martyr's crown. That is only reserved to special saints elected from all eternity to give their life's blood and witness, like the Covenanters, Refomers and those that loved not their lives unto death. Some of us may not attain to the martyr's crown, but thank God we will get the crown if we endure temptation as good soldiers of Christ.

**The second crown you can get is the crown of glory.**

## THE CROWN OF GLORY

Look at I Peter five verses one to four: "The elders which are among you I exhort, who am also an elder, and a witness of the suffering of Christ, (is that not a nice little word. I often wondered whether Peter ever saw the cross. Did you ever wonder about that? Did Peter ever go to Calvary and gaze at Christ? Yes, he did. It says he was a witness of the suffering of Christ. Peter was at the cross) and also a partaker of the glory that shall be revealed: Feed the flock of God which is among you, taking the oversight thereof, not by constraint, but willingly; not for filthy lucre, but of a ready mind; And when the chief Shepherd shall appear, ye shall receive (look at it) a crown of glory that fadeth not away". "A crown of glory".

This is a crown for those who are called to the eldership, who are called to minister to God's people.

Please God, I will obtain that crown as a good soldier of Christ. A crown of glory.

Who gives the crown of glory? Were we not singing about it this morning in the Psalm! Who can give us a crown of glory? Turn over to Psalm twenty-four, and you have a title of Christ in that Psalm. What is He called? He is called The King of Glory. Do you not see it?

The King Eternal, Immortal, Invisible gives you a crown of life.

The King of Glory gives you a crown of glory. "On His head were many crowns". He wears the crown of the King of Glory. And He gives to His people crowns of glory.

**The third crown that we can have, as a believer, is found over in Thessalonians.**

**THE CROWN OF REJOICING**

I Thessalonians chapter two and verses nineteen and twenty: "For what is our hope, or joy, or crown of rejoicing? (here is another crown!) Are not even ye in the presence of the Lord Jesus Christ at His coming? For ye are our glory and joy". And compare that to Philippians chapter four and verse one. And what does it say there? It says: "Therefore, my brethren dearly beloved and longed for, my joy and crown, so stand fast in the Lord". This the soul winner's crown! And those that we win for Christ will be our crown of rejoicing in the day of the Lord's appearing.

Who gives the soul winner's crown?

The first soul winner in the Bible, when the Lord came, will tell you about that.

Turn to John's gospel chapter one. A man called Philip. Do you remember him? He went looking for souls. And he has found Nathaniel. Nathaniel is a very interesting study. He was under a fig tree.

You know in the first of Genesis you have a man under a fig tree; Adam. He is pulling the leaves off to make a garment to cover his sins.

In the first chapter of John you have a man under a fig tree. And Genesis starts off: "In the beginning God created the heavens and the earth". And John's gospel starts off "In the beginning was the Word". And if you study John's gospel you will find days, and if you study Genesis you will find days. There are days mentioned in both of them. And if you work it out there are seven days mentioned in both of them. If you put on your thinking cap and meditate you will find there is a parallel between the days of John and the days of Genesis.

Here is this man Nathaniel. He finds the Lord and what does he call Him? He calls Him "the King of Israel". And if you study carefully you will find that saints of old and saints of new are all reckoned to be the Israel of God.

And it is the King of Israel that gives to us the crown of rejoicing. "On His head are many crowns". He is the King Eternal, Immortal, Invisible. He gives to His people the crown of life. He is the King of Glory, and He gives to His people the crown of glory. He is the King of Israel, and He gives to His people the crown of rejoicing.

**The fourth crown is the crown of righteousness.**

## THE CROWN OF RIGHTEOUSNESS

Do you remember another jailbird; the apostle Paul. He is in prison and he is writing to a young preacher called Timothy. He tells Timothy about another crown. You find it in II Timothy chapter four verse seven: "I have fought a good fight, I have finished my course, I have kept the faith". He was an unrepentant jailbird, he did not make any apologies. Verse eight: "Henceforth there is laid up for me (look at it) a crown of righteousness, (is that only for Paul? Thank God it is not only for Paul) which the Lord, the righteous judge, shall give me at that day: and not to me only, but unto all them that love His appearing". Yes! there is a crown of righteousness for those that love the Lord's appearing!

Who gives that crown of righteousness? Turn over to Hebrews chapter seven and you will find who gives the crown of righteousness: "For this Melchisedec, king of Salam, priest of the most high God, who met Abraham returning from the slaughter of the kings, and blessed him. To whom also Abraham gave a tenth part of all; first being by interpretation the King of righteousness, after that also King of Salem, which is King of peace; Without father, without mother, without descent, having neither beginning of days, nor end of life; made like unto the Son of God; abideth a priest continually". Jesus Christ is the King of Righteousness. So He gives to us the crown of righteousness. "Oh His head were many crowns". He wears the crown of the King of Righteousness. He gives to His people the crown of righteousness.

When did Melchisedec meet Abraham? After Abraham had fought the battle and gained the victory.

When will Jesus give us a crown of righteousness? When we have fought the battle and gained the victory, and when He comes in His Coronation Glory to bring His saints home eternally to the Father's House.

One last thought. We find it in I Corinthians chapter nine and verses twenty-five to twenty-seven: "And every man that striveth for the mastery is temperate in all things. Now they do it to obtain a corruptible crown; but we an incorruptible".

**The fifth crown is an incorruptible crown!**

**AN INCORRUPTIBLE CROWN!**

Who gives us that?

You will find in Revelation chapter seventeen and verse fourteen who gives the incorruptible crown. "These shall make war with the Lamb, and the Lamb shall overcome them: (He gets the mastery) for He is LORD OF LORDS, AND

KING OF KINGS; (He does not fight the battle on His own) and they that are with Him are called, and chosen and faithful". It is the KING OF KINGS who gives us the crown incorruptible!

"On His head are many crowns". He is the KING OF KINGS! He gives us the incorruptible crown.

I trust you have got the import of this message.

**He is the King Eternal, He gives the crown of life,**
**He is the King of Glory, He gives the crown of glory.**
**He is the King of Israel, He gives the crown of rejoicing.**
**He is the King of Righteousness, He gives the crown of righteousness.**
**He is the KING OF KINGS, He gives the incorruptible crown.**

**"AND ON HIS HEAD WERE MANY CROWNS"**

I have three last thoughts for you. You can work them out for yourselves.

There are crowns in the Bible attributed to the Lord, because He is God.

For instance He wears the crown of Creation, because He is God. He wears the crown of Providence, because He is God. He wears the crown of Glory, because He is God. There are crowns *attributed* to Christ!

There are crowns *attained* by Christ. Listen to this. Hebrews chapter two; verse nine: "But we see Jesus, Who was made a little lower than the angels for the suffering of death, crowned with glory and honour". There is a crown He attained to because He was humiliated.

There are crowns attributed to Christ. There are crowns attained by Christ. But there is another one. There are crowns ascribed to Christ! And we have been singing about those crowns today. Ascribing to Him the crowns of glory: The martyrs crown Him. The saints crown Him, for He is the King of saints. The angels of God crown Him. All creation crowns Him. And praise God there is a day coming, if I receive a crown I will not wear it, but I will cast it at His feet. For we read that they cast their crowns at the Saviour's feet. *Ascribed* crowns!

**Crowns attributed to Christ.**
**Crowns attained by Christ,**
**and**
**Crowns ascribed to Christ.**

May we today go in Jesus' Name and strive to obtain that incorruptible crown given us by the KING OF KINGS AND LORD OF LORDS!

THE
# IAN R. K. PAISLEY LIBRARY

## OTHER BOOKS IN THIS SPECIAL SERIES

♦ An Exposition of the Epistle to the Romans

♦ Christian Foundations

♦ Sermons on Special Occasions

♦ Expository Sermons

## AVAILABLE FROM

AMBASSADOR PRODUCTIONS, LTD.

Providence House
16 Hillview Avenue,
Belfast, BT5 6JR
Telephone: 01232 658462

Emerald House
1 Chick Springs Road, Suite 102
Greenville, South Carolina, 29609
Telephone: 1 800 209 8570